To Renda

Rome
Real Estate the Right Way

Here's to your fortune

all the best

Margaret Rome

12-12-08

Real Estate the ~~Right~~ *Rome* Way

Margaret Rome

The Silloway Press

Columbia, MD

Cover design by Marti Garaughty, www.garaughty.com
Printed and bound in the United States of America.

Rome, Margaret. **Real Estate the Rome Way**

LCCN: 2008908998
ISBN-13: 978-0-9802057-9-4
ISBN-10: 0-9802057-9-4

For more information please contact the publisher at
The Silloway Press, 9437 Clocktower Lane, Columbia, MD 21046
301-335-9368 – RETRW@sillowaypress.com – http://sillowaypress.com

For Lee

I made a wish, and you came true.

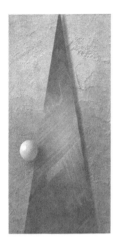

ACKNOWLEDGMENTS

Where to begin? And how to do it without leaving someone out? I could not have written this book or created this career without my family, friends, colleagues, and clients. So many people have taught, coached, encouraged, and cheered me on during this remarkable journey, that all I can do is start where I am and work outward.

Alex Giorgio taught me what it means to be a Type E personality, and from that day on I realized that my whirlwind life is just as it should be. My daughter Erica, who brings her own special gifts to being a Type E, has also enriched my life more than I can say. Peg Silloway, my extraordinary Type E translator, friend, and publisher, manages to make it all look easy.

In real estate, I have made so many friends through the CyberStars®, the Cyber Professionals, ACRE™, and the Real Estate Cyber Society. This list cannot possibly be complete because these relationships continue to begin and grow, but there are some who stand out: Joeann Fossland, Allen Hainge, Anne Hruby, Mike Pallin, Dan Gooder Richards, Floyd Wickman.

I'm grateful for the support of Tom Gimer and Lauren Montillo, TREC (The Real Estate Company of Maryland), and TRAC, home of accelerated marketing. The Maryland Women's Council of Realtors®, NAWBO (National Association of Women Business Owners), and my colleagues at O'Conor, Piper & Flynn and at Coldwell Banker have been there over the years, and I thank you all.

In the last two years there has been no group as much a part of every day as the Active Rain online community. There are hundreds of Rainers who have created connections with me that span the country in all directions. You know who you are, I thank you, and I'm so proud to be part of this extraordinary network of real estate professionals.

There are people who perhaps don't know how important they have been to me, but they have enriched my life: the Monday night poker players, the Saturday morning pilots, the Celebration of Life friends, the Rat Pack, and my LifeBridge buddies.

And now, in no particular order, the many who have touched my life memorably: My mother Frieda Rosenbaum aka Omi, who taught by example "you get by giving." Boo and El, The Treismans, Henry and Marge, Sally, Evie, Dick, Lyl, Terry, Dave, Netsie, Bec and Ben, Gary Sisson, Iris Rombro, Tatiana, Malynda and Rich, Betty and Aaron, Gail Harris, Keith and Kim, April and Marianna, Fred and Jo, Karen Bark, Irene, Linda Norton, Helen Dellheim, Merle, Phyllis and Mort, Joan Brock, Toby Davis, Marty and Elayne, Jay and Alice, Carolyn Howd, Dr. Valentine, Velma, Corie and Vic, Luke and Natasha, Alvin and Nicole, Charlie Brubaker, Keith Whitehead, Anita and Sam, Nelson Zide, Jonathan, Dr. Taub, Marti Garaughty, Lanny and Alma.

Finally, I thank my amazing family: Chet, Kathy, Kim and Kyle, my wonderful Erica, and my life's wish come true, Lee.

PREFACE

Imagine waking up in the morning looking forward to the adventures of the day, knowing that you will have fun and be rewarded, both emotionally and financially. Think what it will be like to have your clients send thank-you notes for helping them buy or sell a house. Picture yourself being congratulated for winning yet another top performer award. I've done all those things, and what I have learned can help you do them, too.

It's true that real estate is one of the most up and down professions anyone can choose. Dealing with that roller coaster takes a strong will and sometimes a strong stomach. Yet there are thousands of real estate agents who hang on tight and enjoy the ride, finding excitement and personal satisfaction in the process of making a living. A few of them even write books to tell other agents how it's done.

Some real estate books I've seen promise a "system" or "formula" for success. This is probably good for some, but it also tends to turn off people who don't want to think or sound like everyone else. I decided there was a book that had not yet been written, one that not only shows how I've had success, but also how taking a personal approach can lead to enormous satisfaction and great fun.

This book is mostly a guide for recognizing the basics and then improvising and using your individual skills and strengths to benefit your clients as well as yourself. Of course you need to keep your eye on the business part, but real estate is more than sticks and bricks — it is also about people and relationships.

If you get that part right, you are well on the way to success. People don't always believe me when I say I work for thank–you notes, my favorite kind of pay. But when I mentor new agents, and they follow my advice while giving it their own personal touch, they learn that an appreciative client means more money, more referrals, and a more rewarding business. What I do is not brain surgery, it's just common sense. The thing is, in real estate and in many other businesses, *common sense is not all that common!*

It all comes down to relationships and learning. In more than 18 years, I've never had a transaction that I did not learn something. And, come to think of it, probably did not have a transaction that I didn't teach something as well.

During booming real estate markets, many people jump into real estate seeing quick, easy money. When the market turns — as it always does — the agents who have taken the time to learn their businesses and build relationships are the ones who not only survive but continue to prosper. My goal for this book is to help you build your successful real estate business with sound principles, the right tools, and a creative approach.

Baltimore, Maryland
September 2008

CONTENTS

INTRODUCTION

> *The frail 80-something lady was burying her husband of many years. Still, she was gracious and composed as friends and family came to see her. She was the mother-in-law of a dear friend, and so I was there, too. It was a terribly sad day and she certainly had reason to be upset, yet she was calm. When my friend complained to her mother-in-law about an unkind comment someone had made, this sweet lady just smiled. "My dear," she said, "don't let unimportant people or unimportant things become important."*

Do you know what is important to you? Over many years in residential real estate, I've learned what's important. And also what to let go of, to put behind me, and to move beyond.

I'm Margaret Rome. I started with no real estate sales experience, but lots of enthusiasm and a thirst to learn; I had my first listing and first sale almost before the ink was dry on my license. The story of how I did that — and all that has followed — is what you'll find in this book.

After successful careers as a pediatric nurse and a ceramic artist, I was fortunate to find my niche in real estate in 1990. It was not a good time to be a new agent. The real estate market in Baltimore, Maryland, was slumping and there were horror stories swirling through the industry of how long it was taking to sell a house. (Sound familiar?) I was new and didn't know better, though, so I ignored what "everybody" knew about the market and proceeded to start listing and selling.

Why should you read this book?

This book is for experienced agents and new agents alike.

You will learn about the personality traits, the approach to problem solving, and the key words I have used successfully to help myself perform at the top of my game every day. (All right, just about every day.) You will learn the strength of WIN, the power of NEXT, and the confidence that results when you DON'T DO UPSET.

By reading this book, you'll learn that anyone can recreate my success using the basic principles and understandings about the business. You will learn about what makes the difference between barely eking out a living and being a top producing agent year after year.

- If you are just thinking about a career in real estate, you will find a good overview of what to expect.
- If you have decided that real estate is right for you and are just starting out, this book will help you make good choices and avoid many of the mistakes that new agents make. It will help you decide where to spend your time, money, and energy as you build your career from the ground up.
- Experienced agents — the good ones — are always looking for new things to learn. Even if you've been in real estate for many years and have survived the ups

and downs of the market, you will find new ideas and perspectives that will help you reach the next level of success.

Here you will find stories that illustrate success strategies as well as some that were learning experiences about what *not* to do. You'll learn the core principles that are the basis of success, and you'll see how they have worked in real life to build a rewarding career. You will see that while you cannot automate success, you can use tools that will help you become a success — a lasting success — in real estate.

That rewarding career will be the result when you combine your desire, dedication, and determination with the principles you will learn in Real Estate the Rome Way.

A final word about words: Real estate has its own language, and that language has different dialects in every state and region of the country. Here in the mid-Atlantic we speak of "going to settlement" or "closing," while on the West Coast people "close escrow," and in the South they "pass papers." Whatever you call it, when all is said and done, a home has changed ownership. The language of real estate in this book is based in Baltimore, Maryland, but the principals apply no matter where you live and work.

This is the kind of book you will want to come back to and reread from time to time. To make that easier, and to reinforce what you learn as you go along, you'll find the key points of each chapter in a summary box at the end of each chapter like the one at the end of this Introduction.

And now...let's get started doing Real Estate the Rome Way!

INTRODUCTION

☐ No matter what careers you have had before, you can become a success in real estate with the right approach based on solid core principles.

☐ There are powerful ideas and habits that will help you build a career in real estate with rewards that include money, of course, but also respect, gratitude, and recognition from your peers and clients.

☐ Whether you are a seasoned agent with many sales to your credit, or are just thinking about getting into the business, this book can be your guide to building a successful career...the right Rome way.

ONE
STARTING OUT THE
~~RIGHT~~ Rome WAY

Why are you here? This isn't one of those "meaning of life" questions. No, what I'm asking is, "Why are you here, holding a book about being a great real estate agent? What do you hope to get out of a real estate career?"

The answers to the question will be as varied as the people they come from:

- Money
- Freedom
- My own business
- Control of my life
- A job
- To meet people
- To have fun
- Recognition
- A retirement income
- To get out of the house
- To work around my family's schedules
- To be my own boss.

Was your reason in there? Real estate can be all that and whatever else you want it to be, provided you do it the right way. There are rules, of course, as there are for every profession. There are laws and regulations specific to your state. And there will be business terms for real estate in your area that will be different in other parts of the country. But there is one constant no matter where you are, no matter how successful you are, and no matter whether you have a shiny new license or you've been in the business for years.

That constant is people. The real estate business is about people. You may learn all the regulations and be able to handle complex documents with your eyes closed, but it always comes back to the people. Buyers, sellers, other agents, brokers, appraisers, lenders, inspectors, and so many more. And friends and relatives of all the above.

Markets go up and down, interest rates rise and fall, but no matter what else is happening, the way you deal with the people will determine how successful you will be. So maybe the first thing you should ask is: "Is real estate for me?"

Is real estate for you?

When you picture your life as a real estate professional and are dreaming about a six-figure income and driving a shiny new luxury car with your custom license plate, it can be hard to take off those rose-colored glasses. So maybe just slip them up to the top of your head long enough for a reality check.

Real estate is a business, and there's a price of admission. You pay in two ways — money and time. That sounds easy enough to understand, right? You spend some money on advertising, spend time selling houses, and you collect a nice fat commission at the end.

Hmm…seems like those glasses slipped down onto your nose, didn't they? Let's look at that again. You spend money to take a real estate course and the exam to get your license. You pay a variety of mandatory fees and licenses each year. You spend money on advertising. You spend money on running your business (computer, phone, gas for your car). Oh yes, and you have to have something to live on until that first commission check comes in — which could be several months.

If you are planning on working at real estate full-time — which is the only way to really make a career of it and do it right — you know, don't you, that "full time" means evenings and weekends? Most people look for houses on the weekends because they work during the week. So the people who help them buy or sell a house also have to be on call on the weekends. And your clients will expect to be able to reach you at any time, day or night. Buying or selling a home is the only thing they are thinking about. It does not matter to them that it is your spouse's birthday or your daughter's piano concert. Your phone will ring.

Still interested? If those last couple of paragraphs made you throw up your hands in horror and say, "I don't want that!" then you should probably put this book back on the shelf. But if you're saying to yourself, "That's no problem. I know how to handle that," then welcome to the wonderful world of real estate done right.

It's true that real estate can be challenging and a bit of an uphill climb at first — but what new adventure isn't? And the climb is so well-rewarded reaching the top. There you will find that good income you've dreamed of, but even more important, you will find great satisfaction. You will be helping people achieve their dreams. What could be better than that? The money and local recognition are nice, but the most lasting rewards come from the people you connect with along the way.

Can you afford to get into the business?

Certainly, you need money to get you through those early

months. In real estate as in any business, it takes money to make money. Depending on where you work, it can cost a few thousand dollars or more in necessary fees and licenses just to be in the business each year. Add to that the cost to take courses that lead to additional professional designations (more about that in Chapter 10), plus the expenses of running your business: advertising, supplies, networking, telephone service, wardrobe, car expenses, and more, and you get an idea of the financial investment involved.

When you start out, you must have some backup income to get you through. Without that, you can fall into one of the first traps you face — financial pressure to get and sell a listing fast. We'll talk more about that particular danger and how to avoid it soon. You need to know that both your living and business expenses are covered from the beginning. Then and only then can you start your real estate career right.

What will you need to spend on during the first few months? As always, expenses will vary depending on your state regulations, the requirements of your broker, and the customs of your particular market. Typical expenditures for your business include:

- Real estate course and books
- Real estate license and board dues
- Errors & Omissions (E&O) insurance
- Multi-function cell phone
- Laptop computer
- Technology expenses such as software
- Compact digital camera
- Website and your own domain name
- Sign name riders
- Print advertising (business cards, brochures, postage, etc.)

Any business has start-up costs, and in real estate it is primarily advertising. Think about it as if you were a storefront business; you need to let people know you exist before they can find you and buy from you. You must build your brand and become known. In real estate you cannot afford to be a secret agent! The most important thing you can do at the beginning is to advertise and to market yourself. If you're saying to yourself, "I'll advertise later when I can afford to," stop. *By the time you can "afford" to advertise, you won't need to any more!*

Before you decide to associate yourself with any real estate company you'll want to ask the broker about costs. Make sure you understand not only what will be required but also what is customary. You don't necessarily have to accept what they offer — negotiate what is included in your split. We'll talk more about this a little later, too.

What if you don't have enough put aside to get in the game right now? Think about what you did when you were a kid and wanted something special — a game, a toy, a car but didn't have the money. Maybe you saved your allowance until you had enough to buy it for yourself. Or you negotiated a loan with your parents. Or you borrowed the money from a bank. These are your answers — save up money, ask friends and family for loans, or borrow from a bank, which includes using your credit card. You have to decide which method fits your comfort zone. Whichever you choose, you *must* have that safety net to support you during the beginning of your real estate career.

But first, wouldn't it be helpful to know if you will do well in real estate, even before you make that commitment? So our next question is…

What type of person will do well in real estate?
Naturally, the answer starts with, "The type of person who will do

well in real estate is the person who loves to work with all kinds of people, likes to solve problems, and gets a kick out of helping people achieve their dreams." That's your basic requirement — being a "people-person." Now add to that being someone who is willing to learn the nuts and bolts of the business, has strong ethics and morals, is a creative thinker, and loves to always be learning something new.

This may sound rather basic, but you have to know yourself and how you work best. Do you approach new situations with anticipation or dread? When someone asks for information, is your first instinct to teach them everything you know, or to just answer the question and get on with what you were doing before they interrupted?

First let me say that you don't have to be a particular personality type to be successful in real estate. But of the many different types of people I've met in the real estate business, some of the most successful agents and brokers seem to share very specific personality traits:

- They are optimistic.
- They can look at a challenge or situation and see more than one solution.
- They hear "It can't be done" and say "Watch me!"
- They tend to go right to the bottom line — they can actually see the end even before they begin.
- They hate routine and details, and have no patience with time-wasting meetings.
- They have a passion for learning something new and sharing what they've learned.
- They want to do things their way and be in control of their world.
- They know what it means to be "in the moment".

That last point is very important; being able to live "in the moment." When I started writing this book, a friend said its title should be WIN, not because I like to win (who doesn't?) but because its an important acronym that works to focus my concentration. It stands for "What's Important Now?"

Sounds simple, doesn't it? But the more you use it — the more you stop and ask yourself "What's Important Now?" — the more you will understand the power of these three words. No matter whether you are planning for the next five years or dealing face-to-face with an irate client, asking and answering this question will help you move forward to success.

In the emotional process of selling and buying a house, you sometimes may feel that you are more an emergency room specialist than a real estate agent. Your seller and buyers are on high alert, and issues quickly become crises. The inspector finds termites! The radon test is positive! Emergency! Panic!

Your clients look to you for help and assurance, and you need to be ready. You need to be able to explain what the issue really means. I tell my clients that there are two kinds of houses in Maryland: those that have been treated for termites, and those that will be. In some parts of the country, every radon test comes back positive. Your job is to be ready with information and mitigation guidance, and then to help your client move on.

Over the years I think I've used more psychology in real estate than I did in nursing. We all get to the point of being totally overwhelmed sometimes, and I believe it happens to new agents more often than others. You have all these buyers and sellers calling you, loads of paperwork, and you're not really sure yet what you are doing. That's when you step back and think, What's Important Now?

During my first year in real estate, it took several months to learn how to deal with it all. I used to grab every phone call, wanting to be available to everyone. But if you take a phone call, then another, then another, you never finish what you were doing when you took that first call. What's important is to handle what you're doing, finish one thing at a time, then move on to the next. Say after me: "There are no emergencies in real estate." No one is going to die if you don't answer the phone. You need to know, **What's Important Now?**

Before cell phones were so widely available and reliable, I had a pager. It was another way to be accessible to my clients and other agents, and at first I equated being accessible with being responsive. Unfortunately, not everyone accepts that there are no emergencies in real estate. One day an agent paged me with the emergency code 911 and I responded right away. The "emergency?" The agent wanted to show one of my properties the following Thursday. I asked, "Why did you put in 911? I'm a nurse, I thought something was wrong with my husband!" She said, "Well, I wanted to be sure you called me back." I threw the pager away.

You cannot keep buyers and sellers from calling you or keep paperwork from piling up. What you can do is control how you deal with the stress. When I do get overwhelmed, when there's just too much going on, one thing that works for me is to pick up the phone and call my husband. I say "I don't have time to talk but I want to tell you I love you." Then I hang up and go on. That puts it all in perspective. **What's Important** *to you* right **Now?**

The Type E Personality

A few years ago I was introduced to a way of looking at personality types that literally changed how I saw myself and the rest of the world. (Don't worry, this is not going to be a scientific discussion of personality types.) One of my favorite getaways is to spend time at Canyon Ranch, relaxing and recharging. You can choose as much or as little activity as you like — just my style. One evening, my husband Lee and I went to a session with Alex Giorgio, who talked about the Type E Personality. Alex identified this personality type during his years as a psychotherapist working with executives, entertainers, entrepreneurs, and high-powered people of all professions. The more he talked, the more Lee kept looking at me, and thinking I had set him up: Alex was describing me to a "T"…make that an "E."

We've all heard of Type A and Type B people. And even though you didn't have a "type" for them, you've also probably known plenty of Type Es. Think of the visionaries — the ones who are always starting new projects but rarely finishing them, and who come up with one crazy idea after another. They seem to have boundless energy. People love to be around them, but spending too long with a Type E can go from exhilarating to exhausting. They have ideas galore and come up with creative solutions to anyone's problems, but they may not be practical. And while you're still thinking about what they said, Type Es are on to the next subject and the next.

During my years in real estate, I've found many agents and other professionals who are Type Es, and they are usually among the top producers. But since part of the purpose of this book is to discuss what I mean by "Real Estate the Rome Way," it has to include a bit about my Type E personality. Stay with me — it will be worth it.

> *That's me — Type E. That's right, I'm a Type E and proud of it. In fact, when I finally understood about Type E, I felt so relieved after years of thinking there was something seriously wrong with me.*
>
> *When I attended that session on Type E, the emotional impact was extraordinary. It was as if a window was thrown open that let in sunshine and a fresh breeze, bird songs and the scent of new mown grass, all the delights of spring and a new start. My crazy way of living turned out to be not only*

> *OK, but a blessing. Now when I look up and see the whirl-wind of my life, I know that's my normal and it's just fine.*

Alex Giorgio developed a quick and fun quiz to see if you have Type E personality tendencies. It takes only a few minutes, and you might see someone you know well in the answers. Of course, there is no right or wrong. This is all about understanding yourself better, and recognizing traits that can be an advantage for a real estate agent. Here we go.

The Type E Quiz[1]

Directions: Please circle **Yes**, **Sometimes** or **No** for each of the following 10 questions.

1.	Do you love starting new projects, especially "impossible" ones?	Y	S	N
2.	Does the thought of having a typical 9-to-5 job make you break into a cold sweat?	Y	S	N
3.	Do you quickly lose interest in a project or job once it is up and running?	Y	S	N
4.	Has delegating responsibility been a major challenge for you?	Y	S	N
5.	When contacted by an old friend you haven't heard from in years, do you immediately pick up where you left off, as if no time has passed?	Y	S	N
6.	Do you love having time to yourself when you can find it?	Y	S	N
7.	Do you usually find small talk a waste of time?	Y	S	N

---

1 Copyright by Alex Giorgio; used with permission.

8.	Do your projects or jobs or romantic relationships usually last between six months and five years?	Y	S	N
9.	Did you grow up feeling that your view of life was different from that of most people?	Y	S	N
10.	Do you consider yourself an intensely passionate person?	Y	S	N

Scoring: Give yourself:
 3 points for each **Yes** answer
 2 points for each **Sometimes** answer
 1 point for each **No** answer.

TOTAL THE POINTS to figure your score.
 My Type E Quiz Score:

Now that you have your score, let's look at what it means.

Type E Quiz Results

Less than 10 points: Replace your calculator battery!

10 - 19 points: You're probably not a Type E.
You may be best suited for a regular 9-to-5 job. You're most likely steady both at home and at work. Follow-through is your middle name. You are an invaluable resource to any company. You also get a purple heart if you have to spend extended periods of time with Type Es.

20 - 30 points: Within the Type E range.
 The higher your score within this range, the greater your Type E tendencies will be. This Type E range is divided into three subtypes:

20 - 23 points: Type E Manager
24 - 27 points: Type E Translator
28 - 30 points: Type E Mystic

Whether you are within the Type E Manager, Type E Translator or Type E Mystic range, all three aspects of the Type E personality are alive and well within you to some degree. While some Type Es can operate from all three modalities simultaneously, there is usually one mode where you will feel most comfortable. This is the one you will find yourself utilizing most of the time.

20 - 23 points: Probably a Type E Manager
You're a practical visionary who, unlike traditional managers, won't shy away from risk. You know how to get the ball rolling and how to keep things on track. Action is your calling card.

The Type E Manager understands that to succeed there is a certain amount of risk one needs to take to move things ahead to the next level. The Type E Managers aren't afraid of risk because they have learned to understand and work with it.

Type E Managers have said that less than seven out of ten failures mean they aren't pushing the "success envelope" enough. Some people say, "If you don't have 20 percent failures, you're not trying hard enough." Striking out with that many failures is part of the process for hitting those remaining three spectacular home runs. Babe Ruth, baseball's home run king, was an exceptional example of this process. Of course, he was also baseball's strike-out king.

24 - 27 points: Most likely a Type E Translator
You're a bilingual visionary who is a vital link between the Type E Mystic, the Type E Manager, and the rest of the world. You excel at being able to think and communicate in two very

distinct styles, both globally and linearly. It's that extraordinary ability to take lofty visions and bring them down to earth that makes you an invaluable — and scarce — resource. The Type E Mystic comes up with the ideas, but needs to make sure to have a trusted Translator such as an attorney to be sure they are legal.

Type E Translators are essential for creating a balanced, successful work, home and school environment for other Type Es. They have an unequaled ability to understand the ideas a Type E Mystic entertains and to effectively communicate them to the rest of the world.

Without a Type E Translator, most Type E businesses and families are destined for continual crisis. Type E Translators appear to be quite rare. If you have one in your group, do whatever it takes to keep them happy, content and well fed.

28 - 30 points: Undoubtedly a Type E Mystic.

You're a mystic visionary who operates so far outside the box you can't remember where the box is most of the time. Since you have more than just your head in the clouds, it can be a challenge to communicate your ideas and passions to other people.

You've also got the gift of time travel — that is, the ability to bring the vision of our world's future into the present. Without you, human experience would be an endless stream of mundane routines, never reaching for the limitless possibilities that you bring to the rest of us.

Type E Mystics have an uncanny ability to see the big picture even before anything can be seen on the horizon. Their challenge lies in dealing with the details and communicating their vision to others. They require the help of a Type E Translator to put their ideas into action and a Type E Manager or two to keep things running smoothly.

When in balance, Type E Mystics are the picture of creativity, enjoying every second of life. Out of balance, they likely will experience a roller coaster ride that creates extreme levels of stress for themselves, their businesses, and their families as well.

. . . . .

This book is about doing real estate right, not about personality types, so I'm going to leave it here with a teaser. At the end of the book, in Appendices A and B, you will find a more detailed discussion of the Type E personality in real estate. If you scored in the Type E range, read these sections for more understanding. In Appendix C is an example of how a Type E operates. If you are — or know — a Type E, these stories will be familiar or frightening, but mostly enjoyable. And if you would like to know more about Type E, email me and I'll be glad to talk more about it with you.

Can a non-Type E be successful in real estate? Of course! Only five to ten percent of the population are Type E. Remember, this exercise is about one personality type I've seen in many top real estate agents, but that does not mean it's required. I also know many agents who are not Type E and are at the top of the profession.

My point is that knowing who you are and what makes you tick just gives you an edge. The best part is that when you know who you are and how you work best, it also gives you that extra confidence that translates into success in every part of your life.

Getting started

All right. You've decided that you really do want a career in real estate. Where do you start?

Before you can work with a buyer or seller and receive your first commission, you need a license — your ticket to ride. There are many real estate courses available for either online self-study or classroom study, whichever works best for you. Some of the major real estate brokerages also have basic courses you can take that will prepare you for the licensing exam.

How do you know which course to choose? Start by asking real estate agents you know for their recommendations, then go online for other options. If you opt for an internet course, be sure you take one that is specific to your state because each state or commonwealth has its own peculiarities.

Once you've taken the course and passed the exam, you need a place to "hang your shingle" — a brokerage with which to associate. How do you choose the right one for you? You want some place where you feel comfortable, where you like the people, and where you feel you will be valued and supported. Talk to people you know in real estate, and go meet with any brokerage you are interested in. Then you choose the one that seems right for you. It's a bit like getting married — that's the easy part; it's staying "married" in real estate that takes work.

Now that you and your license have a "home," you're ready to fly, right? Yes…but. The brokerage you choose will almost certainly have a required course for new agents; the one I took was called "Fast Start." Just as the first course taught you how to pass the exam, your broker's course will teach you how to work in the business. That is a basic for beginning your successful career.

I was lucky to have Anne Hruby as my Fast Start teacher. Not only is she knowledgeable and helpful, she's also able to make real estate understandable and exciting. She helped us through an imposing amount of legal and technical information while keeping us interested and engaged.

With the ink barely dry on my license and the broker's Fast Start course behind me, I enrolled in a program that made an enormous difference in priming me for success. It was a boot camp-type program called Sweathogs from the Floyd Wickman organization. It was intended to get rookies up to speed in a hurry, and did it ever! We worked like crazy, learned a lot, and formed bonds that are still strong years later. Floyd now has a S.M.A.R.T. Selling program and Core Values Club, and holds an annual Master Sales Academy. Wickman training is absolutely the best. Take it and absorb all you can.

One of the important things I learned from Floyd Wickman was that you must find what works best for you and your personality. Every day we had assignments that would teach us techniques and force us to put them to work. We were encouraged to be creative and find solutions that would take us to the desired result even if it didn't follow the assignment.

Here's an example: One of our assignments during the course was to go into the office the next morning and start making phone calls using a criss-cross directory to get our first listing appointment. (These are now all online, but when I started a criss-cross was a massive book that listed addresses and gave you the name and phone number for each one.) We were to make the call, introduce ourselves, and ask the standard, "Are you interested in selling your house now or in the near future?"

That wasn't going to work for me. Talking to people wasn't an issue, but the repetitiveness of the phoning wasn't my style. So instead of using a telephone, I walked my way to appointments. I was already walking around the track at a school for exercise each morning, so now I added more focused conversations. Before long I had listing appointments. Assignment completed, but done my way.

The point is that you can learn and get up to speed quickly; just be sure to make it your own. Obviously, you have to learn the legal and ethical requirements of the profession. You need to know where to go for answers, and you need to understand the processes that your brokerage uses. But your style can and should come through in the way you go about your business of finding clients and helping their dreams come true.

For the seasoned professionals

As someone who has been in the business for a while, you have already learned how to navigate your broker's systems, how to target your advertising, how to talk with potential listing clients, and how to get a deal to conclusion. Now it's time to give a hand to those rookies — time to become a mentor.

Mentoring is one of the most rewarding parts of being in this business. New agents come to the real estate business every day. Some start slowly, some take off so fast all you see is a blur. But each one can use a mentor.

Choosing to be a mentor to a new agent means a commitment of time, and we all have our limits. But it is possible to help someone who wants to learn and who appreciates having one trusted advisor to go to with any question or issue. These days, you don't have to mentor in person. A phone call, an email, or an online forum are some of the ways to help.

> *Floyd Wickman tells a story about a tree cutting contest to see who could cut up the most trees in a given time. Two loggers were out ahead of the others, chopping like mad, building piles of cut up logs. One worked without stopping, furiously cutting and stacking. The other took a five minute break every hour, and working just as furiously the other 55 minutes. At the end, the one who had taken breaks had the larger stack and won the contest.*
>
> *What was the difference? The winning logger took five minutes to sharpen his ax every hour. When he went back to cutting, he worked more quickly and with less effort. For me, mentoring is a way of "sharpening my ax."*

You learn when you teach. Mentoring gives you a chance to sharpen your skills while you help a newcomer. But you must do it because you genuinely want to. The brokerage I started with had a formal "mentoring" program that assigned new agents to more experienced people, and then paid the mentors with a slice of the newcomer's commission. I'm not sure what to call it, but that's not my definition of mentoring.

I love mentoring young agents, and there are plenty of others who feel the same way. Check with your local real estate association to see if they have a mentoring program. There are also virtual and online groups such as the eMentor Connection created by Toby Davis. This group is dedicated to "Educating, Enlightening, Encouraging, Empowering!" and they do it all. It is based on Floyd Wickman's get by giving philosophy, and has proven to be great for the mentors as well as the ones they help.

We'll come back to the theme of you get by giving later. For now, let's get on to the nuts and bolts of the business of real estate the right way.

To summarize, here's what we've covered in this chapter:

CHAPTER ONE - STARTING OFF THE ROME WAY
❑ Understand that you must invest in yourself with time and money to become successful.
❑ Practice asking yourself the WIN question: What's Important Now? It is a technique that will help you throughout your real estate career and your life.
❑ Recognize what kind of personality you are and work with it.
❑ If you are a new agent, seek a mentor. If you are a seasoned professional, become a mentor. Either way, mentoring will improve your chance of success.

TWO
CAN YOU SAY,
"MY REAL ESTATE BUSINESS"?

Go on. Try saying it out loud. "My real estate business." Notice that tingle, that edge of excitement (with maybe a touch of panic) when you combine the words "my" and "business"? Welcome to the world of the entrepreneur!

Real estate is a unique profession because you get to run your own business your way but under the umbrella of a broker. Your business cards, your advertisements, and your yard signs will have your name but they will also the name of your broker. In Maryland and most states, you will sign an agreement as an independent contractor to represent the broker. If you've chosen wisely, that broker has a good reputation and supports your business by providing an office location, training, support services, and a network of other agents you can work with. In return, the broker receives part of every commission you earn. Because of this it can be easy to fall into the illusion that you work *for* the broker.

Don't do it! Do not ever forget that you are an entrepreneur and that everything happens because *you* make it happen. It is exciting and scary, yes, but it is ultimately so rewarding to be in absolute control of your company's future success. It's also something to think about seriously before you get too far into the business.

We've already talked about the characteristics that make a good real estate professional — like optimism and passion and the ability to ask "**What's Important Now?**" — and they also apply to making a successful entrepreneur. There are other traits a business owner needs. Here are some other questions to help you analyze your entrepreneurial outlook. Just keep in mind that while it is your business, there is nothing that says you have to do it all yourself.

- **Am I really a self-starter?** Yes, we all want to think we are, but no one is listening now, so be honest. In your real estate business, no one will be looking over your shoulder and reminding you to get your ads placed on time.

- **Can I tolerate the level of detail needed to run the business?** I'm not talking about the details you need to fill out a contract or put a property in the multiple list. I mean will you collect receipts for supplies you buy, track expenditures, and make your tax deposits on time? Yes, you can pay to have these done, but it's up to you to see that they are done and on time.

- **Does flexibility come naturally to me?** Entrepreneurs have an enormous advantage over larger businesses because they can "turn on a dime." When a new opportunity comes knocking on the door, the entrepreneur can invite it in, pour the coffee, and sign the contract before the big company can even convene a committee to study it.

- **Do I have the resources to get from startup to success?** OK, I'm sneaking this one in under a different name, and yes we did talk about it in Chapter 1. That will tell you how important it is. Any business must start out with enough capital to support the enterprise until money starts to flow in. And lack of capital is the number one reason small businesses fail. If you were selling laptops or 747s, you would have to put money out to buy inventory, advertise your wares, take the orders, and ship them, before you got the first dollar back. It's the same with real estate, but instead of laptops and airplanes you have to build an inventory of listings before you can sell them and start to see money flowing back in your direction.

Master real estate trainer Anne Hruby reminds her students that, even though we have to work for a broker, we're still our own boss. In the first class, Anne asks her students, "Why do you want to become a real estate agent?" The most common answer she receives is, "I was tired of working for someone else. I want to be my own boss and earn a lot of money."

Later in the course, when students have been working in real estate for a while, Anne asks, "Do you like your boss?" She says, "It is important that you like who you become."

Then she asks the class, "Would you hire you as a real estate agent? If so, why? And if not, why would anyone else?"

Simple questions can lead to some very important answers.

I suspect you're starting to get antsy by now. I promised to talk about being a real estate agent, and so far all we've covered is the boring business stuff. When do we get to the fun? Soon, I promise. Think of this as the warm up stretches before you go on the treadmill.

Buyers and sellers and teams, oh my!

Most people start out just happy to have any clients they can get.

It's good experience to work with both sellers and buyers for a few months. That way, you get a good sense of the issues that are important to both, and you start to recognize the questions that come up all the time and how best to answer them.

Soon, though, you'll have an idea of which you prefer to work with. As an agent, you can choose to focus on sellers or buyers, and you can either work alone or as part of a team. Of course you don't have to narrow your scope, but it is an option.

Listing agents work primarily with people who want to sell their home. The listing agent represents the seller and has the interests of the seller always as a first consideration. Sometimes called the seller's agent, a listing agent needs to make sure the seller is qualified to sell, acts on behalf of the seller to show the house to potential buyers, and works with the seller to come to agreement with the buyer on terms that will sell the house. A listing agent may see one or many potential buyers before finding the right one.

A buyer's agent works to find the right home for people who are ready to buy, regardless of whether they have a home to sell or not. Here, the attention is on learning the truth about what buyers want and finding the home that comes closest to meeting their wish list. Being a good buyer's agent requires first qualifying the buyer — verifying that the buyers have the financial resources needed — then knowing your area well so you can help a buyer find the right combination of location and price. A buyer's agent also helps negotiate the terms of a contract to get their clients the best possible deal. Where there are differences, the good buyer's agent will work with the seller's agent to learn what's important to each side and find areas where a compromise can be worked out that makes everyone happy. Buyer's agents have a specific contract with clients making it clear that they are taking the buyer's position and looking out for their interests.

Agents who work with buyers do get around a lot! And flexibility is key. Buyers are thinking day and night of their hunt for the perfect home, and when they see an ad that sounds like just what they are looking for, they will want to see it *now*. Buyer's agents go with their clients to view potential properties so that they can ask questions their clients may not think of.

Not too long ago, a real estate agent was always a solo act. But in the last few years, the concept of a team of agents has taken hold. In a team, there is one lead agent and a few or many associates who work together as a team under the leader's banner. A team may consist of real estate agents as well as people who manage the team's office, contract paperwork, and transaction processing. The team may work within an established brokerage firm, or the team may establish their own brokerage.

Being part of a team has many attractions, especially for someone just starting out. But I've always known that my choice is the solo route as a listing agent. It is possible that choice may have restricted my earning potential, but I don't believe so. It certainly does limit the number of listings I can have at any one time, but that suits my style, too. By limiting my listings to no more than 15 at a time, I am able to give the kind of service that has been key to my success. Part of it is that I am your basic control freak. I answer my own phone, make my own appointments, and as much as possible do my own showings, then shepherd each deal along to completion. By working directly with my clients I learn more about what they really want and can work to get them just that. In the end, I believe it not only saves time but also leads to happier clients and smoother deals.

Being a listing agent has also made me a superb buyer's agent. I know what to look for and what to put in a contract. When I choose to be a buyer's agent, for example when I have sold a client's home, there is no one who can serve that client better.

It's a matter of control

Every once in a while, when I'm talking with another real estate agent, the subject of appointments comes up. When I say that I always — yes, always — make my own appointments, I can almost predict what will happen. The eyes widen, the brow furrows, there's a quick intake of breath, and then, "You're kidding!"

No, I'm not.

"But doesn't it waste your time?" they ask.

Showing the wrong house to the wrong buyer, that wastes my time. Making my own appointments saves time and aggravation for me and my listing clients. How can this one task make a big difference? Here are just a few of the issues that I can — and do — clear up before I show a listing to a potential buyer. And yes, I've actually had all of these and more:

Mismatches

The condo restricts pets.	The buyers have a dog and a cat. No, you can't sneak them in.
The prospective buyer is 93 years old	The unit I have listed is on the top floor. Oh, and there are no elevators.
The condo has no balcony.	The buyer has claustrophobia.
It is a lovely penthouse unit.	The buyer is afraid of heights.
The buyer is restricted to a wheel chair.	My listing is a split-level house.
The family wants all bedrooms on the same level.	The house is a Cape Cod.

Missing Information

The buyers haven't talked to a lender yet because they want to wait until they find something they like.	*Do you think it's likely I could be showing them houses they can't afford?*
I have a co-op listed. The by-laws require the unit must be purchased for cash — there can be no mortgage.	*If we haven't discussed this first, it would be no surprise when the buyer asks if the monthly fee "includes the mortgage payment."*
My client's condo has high monthly fees.	*The prospective buyer didn't ask before seeing the property (and his agent didn't tell, obviously). Then he asks if we can negotiate the fees down along with the price. Um...sure, right along with the property taxes.*

And then there are the "must haves":

It must have an attached garage – it's safer that way.

> *No, that's too dangerous, the garage has to be separate.*

The fireplace must be wood burning.

> *The fireplace must be gas. No fireplace – it's not safe.*

Must have a swimming pool.

> *Absolutely no swimming pool!*

The house must be on a main road with sidewalks and nearby neighbors.

> *No, the house must be secluded, away from prying neighbors.*

The townhouse kitchen has to be at the front so I don't have to schlep groceries through the house.

> *Who wants a kitchen at the front? We need a kitchen in the back so we can walk out on the deck.*

And on and on. You get the idea. There are so many ways that well-meaning home sellers and prospective buyers can waste their time and energy. Over the years, I've learned that the one best way to eliminate these issues is to make my own appointments and ask the questions up front. That way I can assure my sellers that I will only bring qualified buyers into their home.

You might have noticed that I said a while back that you don't have to do everything yourself, just make sure that it gets done, and done right. Add that concept to the choice of being a solo agent, and you come to my solution: working solo *with a team*. When I need specific help with a specific job, I call on someone from my group of trusted professionals. It's a solution that works well for me, and we'll talk more about it in Chapter Seven. For now, let's summarize and then move on to Brand YOU.

CHAPTER TWO - CAN YOU SAY, "MY REAL ESTATE BUSINESS"?
❏ When you are a real estate agent, you are an entrepreneur — a self-starting business owner who has the flexibility and resources needed for success. You make everything happen.
❏ You can choose to work with buyers only, sellers only, or with both.
❏ There are advantages to being part of a real estate team; working solo also has advantages, especially if you work solo but with a team you can call on for specific tasks.

THREE
WHOSE FACE IS THAT?
IT'S BRAND YOU!

No matter where you hang your license, and whether you choose to work with a team or fly solo, your first priority will be creating and marketing your brand. That's *you*.

Think about every real estate ad you have ever seen. What's the first thing you notice? Besides the listings and photos of houses, there is always a face to go with the name of the agent. They may be smiling or somber, young or not so young, but there is always a photo. "But I look terrible in pictures!" I can hear you, but it doesn't matter. As someone once said, they're going to find out that you're not Miss America or Mr. Universe anyway! So go get some photos taken of yourself, choose the ones you like best, and use them for all your marketing materials. If you are not willing to put your face in front of the public, it is time to rethink whether you really want to be in the real estate business.

Whether it's an ad for a team of agents or one individual, an agent's name will probably be repeated several times. The purpose, obviously, is to build name recognition. The more people see your name and your face, the more familiar and trusted you will become, even to people who do not actually know you and haven't even met you yet.

Think about your local TV weatherperson. If you've been watching the news for several months and have seen the weather forecaster chatting with the anchors and the sports caster, you can start to feel that you know him as an individual. Now suppose he knocks on your door late one night and says he's got a flat tire; his cell phone is dead, and asks to use your phone. Do you invite him into your house, ask him to sit down, and offer him coffee? Wouldn't you be more likely to do that for the personality you "know" than someone you don't know?

Of course, you don't really know him or anything about him. But you've seen him so often that there is a feeling of familiarity and comfort so you're willing to have him come into your home and be with your family.

That's the power of advertising and of building brand recognition. Your brand...YOU.

Brand Building 101

OK, you accept that building Brand YOU is important to your success as a real estate agent. How do you do it?

This is going to sound too simple, but it's true. You put your name and face on everything, you tell everyone what you do, and you do it repeatedly and consistently. By your actions you establish a reputation for ethical personal service, and you consistently deliver the service you promise.

When John Nordstrom opened his first shoe shop in Seattle in 1901, he determined that his business would be based on exceptional service, selection, quality, and value. Today, if you ask a shopper why they like Nordstrom's, you'll probably hear those same words. That's brand building.

There will be many items in your promotion kit; an "elevator speech," a tagline, a Website, a Weblog, business cards, print advertising, perhaps promotional items, mailings, and personal notes. Throughout all of these you will want to have a consistent appearance and a consistent, unique message.

The Elevator Speech. You've probably heard this term, but just in case; an elevator speech is a short, simple, persuasive statement about what you do that you can repeat (without sounding as if you're reading it!) in 10 to 30 seconds. The idea is to have something ready to go when you step into an elevator and find yourself face to face, and alone, with the one person who can become your best, most important, and most influential client. For an actor, it might be Steven Spielberg. For a real estate agent, how about a top pro football player who has just signed with your team and you know will need to move to your town? Or perhaps the CEO of a major company that has just acquired a competitor and will be needing relocation services for dozens of employees who will be transferring to your town in the next six months? You can't just smile and look away. You have only seconds to make your point, but you can't come on like a hungry shark. With an elevator speech ready to go, you have a chance to make the right kind of impression and open a door for yourself.

So what goes into your elevator speech? The first step is to craft one sentence that sums up what you do and yet leaves a space for someone to ask for more. Start by thinking about what it is you do, and after you get past "I list and sell houses," which is the same thing every other real estate agent does, think about the *results* of what you do. Focus on the benefits, not on the mechanics. Instead of "I help people get the best price for their home," you could say, "I make real estate dreams come true." The first version is simple and true, but doesn't start a conversation. The second version raises a bunch of questions; What dreams? How do you make them come true? Work it over until you find the words that come comfortably to you, that fit your style.

Once you have the basic, simple statement, take that sentence and expand it to fill 10 seconds. Then when you have one you're happy with, expand it to 30 seconds. Practice them with everyone you talk to. Is it working? What kind of reaction are you getting? Tweak your statements until you're comfortable and they are second nature. Now you have your Elevator Speech. You'll use it at every networking event you go to, every conference you attend. You'll hear other people's versions and maybe find something you like and can adapt to yours. Have some fun with it, see how creative you can be, how memorable you can make it, without losing the central idea...Brand YOU.

The Tagline. Most businesses that you recognize have a short, memorable statement that gets plastered on everything. These are the lines you see with the ™ or ﹖ sign after them, meaning they are trademarks or service marks.

You need a tagline, too. You will add it to your business card, your advertising, and when time is short, you'll use it as your instant elevator speech.

> *You know how it goes. You are at a networking event or business association meeting, and it's that time when everyone gets to introduce themselves. The leader says, "Give us your name, company, and a little about what you do...and keep it short!" People get up and some drone on and on, others barely whisper their name and stammer through a description.*
>
> *When my turn comes, I say my piece in three seconds flat and sit down while they are still laughing and applauding.*
>
> *"Margaret Rome. Sell your home with Margaret Rome."*
>
> *Works every time, people remember, and yes, I do get business from it!*

My tagline started as "Market your home with Margaret Rome." But a business advisor said to me, "People don't want their homes marketed. They want them *sold!*" Replacing that first word changed the focus of the line and gave it a good verbal rhythm. In six words I say who I am and why you want me as your real estate agent.

So how do you come up with a tagline? Start with your name. Can you relate it to real estate, to how you do business, or can you make it sound like a well known (and well thought of!) product or person? Try thinking of logical connections and rhymes. Suppose your last name is Crane, try something like "Get a lift in life with Crane." For a husband and wife, "Spouses sell houses." Perhaps your name would also lend itself to a memorable rhyme. No, I didn't marry Lee Rome so I could have a great tag line, but it was a nice extra! After all, "Sell your home with Margaret Rosenbaum" just doesn't cut it.

If neither your first or last name lends itself easily to a tagline, think about what sets you apart from other agents. Is it your locale? Do you have the good fortune to live in a place that the rest of the world considers paradise? There's a start. What if your locale is known for one special feature? Ken Deshaies is a Realtor® in Breckenridge, CO. His Snow Home Properties uses the tagline, "Snow place like home." Short and memorable…perfect!

Don't worry if you have trouble coming up with the perfect tagline. Write down several possibilities. Say them out loud. Try them out on your friends and in networking; what kind of reaction do you get? Always listen to suggestions, and feel free to contact me if you need help with a tagline (mrome@homerome.com).

The Website. You cannot be in real estate today without a professional Website. Period. These days, some 84 percent of buyers go to the Internet[1] to research homes and neighborhoods. Sellers go online to find out about real estate agents and brokers. If you

---

1 National Association of Realtors®'s report for 2007

don't have an attractive, useful, and easy-to-navigate Website, you will be invisible to your potential clients. But having a Website without driving traffic to it is like having a billboard in the middle of the desert.

There's been a lot of talk about how the Internet is changing real estate. Back when word processors first made work easier and more efficient, some people refused to give up their trusty electric typewriters. While the rest of the business world moved ahead, they were typing and retyping, struggling with carbon paper and Wite-Out®.

It's the same with the Internet. For years, real estate agents and brokers guarded listing information and doled it out after qualifying prospective buyers. When the Internet started to make information available, some agents saw it as a threat and resisted using the new technology. But those Realtors® who could see the potential of easy access to listing information are the agents who are growing and thriving. In fact, because consumers are now doing a lot of the work themselves, these Realtors® can concentrate on building relationships, creative marketing, and becoming valued professionals who can help sellers and buyers through the complex process of getting to the settlement table.

Brad Inman of Inman News, while moderating a panel discussion, said, "It's not that the Internet is going to get rid of Realtors®, it's going to get rid of Realtors® that don't use the Internet."

I love this quote! I use the Internet extensively with my Website, my blog, and email. It's one of the reasons I can accomplish so much as a solo agent.

You should have a Website that you control, and not rely on a site created by your broker. You should also have your email through your own site. This means you need your own URL or domain name — the Internet address that reads www.Your-Name.com. It costs only about $10 a year to maintain a domain name, so don't even think of skimping. Consider buying several versions of your name. Malynda Madzel, a good friend and business colleague, as soon as she heard I was going into real estate said, "Your Website has to be HomeRome!" She was right. For instance, I also own www.HomeRome.com, www.SellYourHomeWithMargaretRome.com, www.MargaretRome.com, and dozens more, including my phone numbers.

It is easy to have any domain name you own direct traffic to any other domain name. For instance, if someone types "margaretrome.com" into an Internet browser, it will bring up my Website. What they don't see is that in the background I have set it up so that any traffic that goes to margaretrome.com is automatically forwarded to homerome.com. That way I never miss a potential visitor because they don't know the name of my Website, but they do know my name or phone number.

So it's a given that you need a Website. How do you get one? Take the time to visit other Realtor® Web sites and think about what you like. Then use your network of friends and colleagues to ask for recommendations on good designers and developers. Look for a Website developer who can take your ideas about design and create the look you want. If you make a list of features you want and don't want, and provide a list of URLs for sites you particularly like, it will make the job easier for your Web designer and also make if more likely that you will get what you want. A good place to start looking at outstanding real estate sites is the CyberStars®. (You'll read more about this group in Chapter 9.) You will need to provide the content — the words on the Web pages — which you can either write yourself or have done for you.

How much will it cost? The answer is, of course, that depends. It depends on what content and features you want on your site, how frequently the content will change (for instance, when you take new listings or sell a property), and whether you will maintain the site yourself or have someone else do it for you. We'll get into more detail about what makes a good real estate Website in Chapter 9.

The Email Address. This one is simple. Your email address should be YourName@YourWebSite.com. If you don't have your own email address, you don't have control over your own future. Super real estate trainer Joeann Fossland puts it this way:

> *The most important action an agent can take to create their online presence is a permanent email address. Obviously, if you are a professional, a free Hotmail or Yahoo address doesn't send a powerful message. Even YourName@Your-Broker.com does not give you the benefit of either being a permanent address or branding you. What if your company gets purchased or you change companies? If you are using an address at one ISP (Internet Service Provider) and decide to change services, you have to tell everyone of your new address. Do you think possibly you might lose some people or business by doing that?*
>
> *You need an address that will never change because you own it. Then it can be forwarded to whatever ISP you use. Buy a domain name or begin to use the domain you already have. This will brand you with every mail you send out. Buy your name or the name that describes your business: YourFirstName@YourFirstLastName.com or YourFirstName@Move2YourCity.com . Regardless of which way you choose to go, the most critical thing is that now YOU own the domain name.*

Joeann is right. Using your broker's email service puts you in a precarious situation. Suppose you join a brokerage as a new agent. You like everyone and everything about the broker: you are treated fairly, supported, and appreciated. Over the first five years, you build up an impressive list of contacts and email addresses. Then one day the brokerage is sold. All of a sudden, your email address changes from You@OldBroker.com to You@NewBroker.com. When this happens, all the emails you had at OldBroker.com are gone. Worse, over the next few months you find that you don't really like it with NewBroker and decide to find a new home for your business. You change brokers and now your email is You@NextNewBroker.com, and now they are gone again.

Do you suppose a client you worked with a year ago will be able to find you? When the email they send you comes back as un-deliverable, what are the chances they will try to track you down? Worse, do you still have all your email addresses, or were they lost in the shuffle? If your contact list is attached to your broker's email server, all that valuable information can disappear in an instant.

The solution is simple. Have all email forwarded to your own address. Yes, your broker will give you an email address; all you have to do is have the broker set up the forwarding (this is a common request, easily done). Then, no matter where you are, your email address will never change. And that client who liked you so much when you sold their house three years ago will be able to find you when they're ready to move up next time.

The Weblog (Blog). You recall that 84 percent of home buyers go to the Internet first and start their search for both homes and Realtors® there? Your Website is one way they can learn about you, but it is not the only — or even the best way. Today, having a blog is as important as having a Website. Make that an *active* blog. If you haven't been plugged in to the world of blogging, now is the time to get started. A blog is an online journal that you update frequently.

When you have a blog, you can not only speak to your prospective clients but actually also carry on electronic conversations with them. This is the place to let people know what kind of person you are, how you deal with people, and what they can expect from you. Of course, your Website has your biography and awards and the certifications and designations you have earned. But it probably does not tell people about your interests, your attitudes, and how you spend your time.

The point of a Weblog is that you can let people become comfortable with you. Recall what I said at the beginning about branding and how people can come to feel they know you? A blog is a very effective tool in creating that feeling of familiarity.

The one important thing to know about blogging is that it is *not* advertising. It is a place for you to demonstrate your knowledge of your market, to give advice, and to comment on what's happening in your area. (We'll have a more thorough discussion of blogging in Chapter 9.) For now, just know that you need to have this low- or no-cost feature in your brand-building plan.

Print Advertising. Since I'm emphasizing how important it is to have a Website and a blog, does that mean you don't need to advertise your listings in the local newspapers, too? You'll hear plenty of opinions on both sides of this question. Many agents feel that the Internet is the only place you need to advertise because so many potential buyers go there to research. They don't believe people settle in with the real estate section of the Sunday paper and read all the ads. It's true that people in their 30s, and 40s who are buying houses will most likely go directly to the Internet. But I still believe in the value of having potential clients open the paper and see my face, name, and listings.

Call me old-fashioned, but I do both print and Internet advertising. I know that not everyone who buys a house — or who is helping someone look for a house — is in their 30s. There are other generations and they do read newspapers, and they do need print ads. This generation includes people with lots of disposable income who are looking for nice homes. It also includes people with children and grandchildren who may need a new home, and these parents have time to help their kids with the search. Why would you ignore an entire group of potential clients by refusing to talk to them in the way that will reach them? Sure, many of them are tech savvy, but they often find us on the Web *after* seeing our names and faces in newspapers, in glossy magazines, or hearing us on the radio.

It's true that many potential buyers start a home search on the Internet before they ever contact a Realtor®. But that doesn't mean that just having a Web presence is enough, any more than doing the Three Ps is enough: placing the listing in the multiple list (which is *not* the same as advertising on the Web, though some agents think so), placing a sign in the ground, and praying — these won't sell houses.

For me, knowing the market, taking the time to listen and learn about the client's needs, working my wide network of connections and resources, investing my time and talent in each transaction, and yes, placing ads in all appropriate media, that sells houses. Sure, you can Google me and my properties anytime. I'm there. But I'm also in various media depending on location.

Some sellers like to see their home in the paper, others love to see it on their computer. Whether it's a big ad on your Website or a print ad in the local paper, how can it be wrong to do whatever it takes to reassure your sellers that you are marketing their home?

Promotional Pieces. You will hand out and/or mail a lot of paper as a real estate agent. You will have business cards, information sheets for each property, perhaps postcards, and other items. They will all have your name and tagline on them, along with your phone number, Website URL, and email address. And you will notice that just about every other agent is doing the same thing. How do you make your pieces stand out from the crowd and draw the right kind of attention?

Obviously, you don't do what everyone else does. Instead of post cards I use stationery — personal note size, not business — with my MRome signature and Sell Your Home With Margaret Rome printed on it. Also, I have a rubber stamp with my MRome signature and return address.

For listings, I make up flyers with glossy photos and the special selling points of the property, and my contact information. (I started doing this in the days before Internet, but flyers still work.) I print up copies and give them to the sellers to spread around and also to leave out during an open house. These days, the flyers are separate pages on my Website that buyers, agents, and sellers can print out. Buyers can carry them with them; agents can print them to hand to a potential buyer. And the seller won't run out of flyers because they can print them right off their computer. The idea still works.

As for business cards, I have customized them for each listing. I print information about the listing on one side and my information on the other. I didn't use the cards provided by any brokerage I have worked with, even though they were free, since they promoted the company. Instead, I have my own design printed with my name and MRome signature logo. Never forget that it is *your* business and *your* name you need to promote.

What about the calendars and refrigerator magnets and other give aways? Nope, never used them. I knew from the beginning that I wanted my reputation to be for personal service and attention. I didn't want to be known as the "agent with the cute magnets" or "the one with the flashlight key chains." When I want to give a client something, it's a personal gift and one I choose for them, even if it's just a token, something to say, "I was thinking of you."

> *An older lady whose house I sold has bad circulation. Her feet are always cold. One day I saw the "World's Softest Socks" — they were cushy and fuzzy and warm. So I bought a couple of pairs and sent them to her. She still talks about that simple little gesture and how much it meant to her.*

Building Brand YOU takes some time, but it will pay dividends throughout your career. Take every opportunity to create a positive image for you and your real estate business. In fact, try for what is my idea of the perfect compliment: "You don't seem like a real estate agent!"

But let me make this clear: If you are serious about being in this business, you need to spend money up front for personal promotion. If you don't believe you can make that money back, then you need to rethink being in real estate.

Coming up next — getting that first listing and sale.

CHAPTER THREE - WHOSE FACE IS THAT? IT'S BRAND YOU!
❑ A key to your success in real estate is building Brand YOU: making your name and face well known in your community.
❑ Brand building includes your elevator speech, tagline, Website, email, advertising, and marketing materials.
❑ Remember that you want to build YOUR brand, not your broker's. When choosing your brand building tools and techniques, make sure you use the ones that work best for you, not just those that "everyone" says you "ought to." You're not everyone…you are Brand YOU.

FOUR
LISTING, LISTING,
WHO'S GOT THE LISTING?

There you are, license in hand, basic training under your belt, with your Brand YOU established, ready to take on the world and show what you can do. But what's the best way to get that first listing?

Many new agents start with the traditional cold calling and floor duty. By now you probably can guess that I have my own take on how to do those things successfully. As with everything in your real estate business, you need to approach listings in the way that works best for you.

When I started in real estate it was just something to do while I recovered from an automobile accident. The doctors ordered me not to lift anything heavy...ha! At the time I was a professional potter. The boxes of clay I used for my pottery weighed 50 pounds each. Working with clay is heavy physical exercise — lifting the clay, slapping a lump of it on to the wheel, shaping the dense clay as the wheel spins, drawing it up and out with one hand on the inside of the vessel and one on the outside, pressing together to move the clay without distorting the shape, all while hunched over a spinning wheel. Obviously, I couldn't do any of that while I healed, but I needed *something* to do.

That's when I found real estate. I was already helping friends and neighbors write ads to help them sell their homes. So while I healed, and until I could get back to my pottery, I thought I'd give real estate a try.

The key was that I approached it as a learning experience, something new to master, and *not* as a live-or-die situation. I went after each listing as if I didn't need it. I did floor duty just to learn how to use the phones and did get some business from it. When someone called to see a house, I always gave the calls to the listing agent, or I took the information and called the agent with it. (Unfortunately, that's not what most people do.)

It's interesting how things come around. Even though it's been years, former agents remember my willingness to help when they were in real estate, remember how I work, and I have become the agent they use when they or friends or family are ready to sell.

Cold calling was not something I would do — you'll recall I said in Chapter 1 that I walked my way to appointments during my morning exercise at the local school. You can do the same thing by taking the purpose of the assignment — cold calling for appointments — and matching it to what you do or can do easily. I even used to turn telemarketing calls into my own sales calls, too. For instance, when someone called to clean my chimney (which I don't have), I said, "Sure, if you can find one, you can clean it!" This kind of impromptu banter helped me be a better salesperson. Remember, there's never only one way to make things happen. The right way is what works for you.

When trying to get listings, especially in the early days, it's easy to get too focused on paperwork and numbers. Yes, they are important, and you have to get them right. But there are people in your broker's office who can help you and who will review what you've done on the documents. Think of those piles of papers and intricate calculations as the evidence. But remember the main event is your interaction with your clients and prospects. This is a people business, and you will do best if you work with people you like. Yes, that's not always practical, but it should be your goal. From the beginning you must feel that you are the best person for that client.

When I list somebody's house, I really do feel that I'm doing something for them, not that they are giving something to me. I've heard agents say things like, "Do you believe my next door neighbor didn't give me their listing?" "Do you believe my girlfriend listed with somebody else?" As if somehow neighbors and friends owe it to them! Nobody gives you anything in this business — why should they? You didn't earn it — and you didn't lose it because you never had it in the first place.

Getting that first listing

My first listing came on a dare. Remember that I was green, that I didn't yet know the "right" way to do things, and that I had the attitude that I did not *need* the listing…so what could I lose?

> When I started in real estate my husband, Lee, had just accepted the position of CEO in a local company. He was replacing "Bob" whose contract was not being renewed.
>
> One day Lee said to me, "Bob's got to sell his house, why don't you call him?"
>
> It was a dare, and I took it. I picked up the phone and called, and said "Hi, Bob. Congratulations on your retirement. By the way, you know I'm in real estate now, if I can help you sell your house, I'm available." Bob slammed down the phone. And Lee laughed. He figured that's what would happen.
>
> This was just a week before the company picnic, and I asked Lee if Bob would be at the picnic; he said, "How do I know?"

So I said, "Watch this!" I picked up the phone, dialed Bob, and said, "Hi Bob, this is Margaret, do not hang up on me! Are you coming to the picnic on Sunday?" He said he didn't know. And I said, "I need you to make me one promise: Do not list your house with anyone until you speak to me on Sunday." And I hung up.

I don't know where I got the chutzpah to do that, but I had nothing to lose. What was he going to do? My husband already had his job. But I knew that Bob, a tough, ornery guy and the father of five girls, liked strong women.

At the picnic on Sunday, Bob held court at a picnic table while, one after another, everyone in the company came over to wish him well. And all the time I was sitting at the same picnic table with him and trying to tell him why he should list his house with me.

Bob had three questions for me:

1. *"Why in the world would I ever list a house with you? You've never sold a house before!"*
2. *"You don't know my neighborhood, you don't even know where it is."*
3. *"The people who live across the street from me are the real estate agents who sold the house to me, why would I use you?"*

At one time, Bob had kiddingly offered me a position at the company and I told him then he couldn't afford me. And later when he did actually make me an offer, I turned it down, saying the offer wasn't enough. So now I said, "First, you're right, Bob, I've never sold a house, but you know I can sell." Then, "The reason you should list with me is that you're the only listing I have. I am either going to make or break my career on you. I have nobody else's house to show, you can have all my advertising dollars, and I'll be there for you.

I have an entire company that wants to watch me succeed."

Second — well I never answered him about the neighborhood and the people across the street. But before I left I did say that I wanted an answer from him by Tuesday.

Sure enough, on Tuesday Bob called telling me to be at his house. I called my then-manager and said, "Meet me at the house and bring the paperwork!" I had never done a listing, never done a sale, had no forms; I didn't even know what I was supposed to bring to a listing interview.

At the house Bob challenged me, "How long is it going to take you to sell my house?" Now to me, that's a buying question, a strong indication he'd already bought into me.

My answer was, "How long will it take you to get this house into show condition?"

That set him back and he got upset with me. "What do you mean?"

"I can't sell this house with orange shag carpet. Here's the name of my carpet person, here is the color you should order, and as soon as the carpet work is done, we can put it on the market. In the meantime, I'd like to measure and photograph the house." Where did I get that? I still can't tell you, but it was the right response. And yes, I had the name of someone I knew to do the carpet work.

Bob said I couldn't go upstairs then — another buy signal. "OK." I said, "but we have to do the paperwork. What do you want for the house?"

He responded, "This is what I want to clear," and he gave me the amount. I took that number and added closing costs and commission to it, showed him the total and said, "I think I can get more than this for the house, but this will give you the amount you want to clear. If we do that, will you be satisfied?"

"I don't want to get any more for it," he said. "I want to be fishing this summer in upstate New York." Given that it was already July, that told me time was an important part of his decision. So we agreed on an asking price and I filled in the listing agreement. He didn't ask about the commission rate since we had agreed on his bottom line amount, and he signed the listing. We agreed I could come back in a couple of days to measure, we shook hands, and my manager and I left.

Outside my manager stopped and shook his head. "I don't believe you!"

I said, "What do you mean?"

"You got a full commission."

"Did I do something wrong?"

"You didn't discuss the commission."

"There was no reason to discuss the commission."

"I've never seen anybody take a listing without discussing commission."

"It was a done deal. The commission was never an important part of it, only what I could put in his pocket."

My manager was just floored. In my ignorance, I didn't know you could cut or not cut the commission. I didn't know any better, and so I had my first listing with a full 7 percent commission.

Later, my manager got a call from those "seasoned" agents across the street who had originally sold Bob the house. They complained about me, that I had priced the house too low, that I was hurting the market (and it was not a "good" market at the time, though I didn't know that, either) by pricing the house too low. But I was selling for the seller, and this was what the seller wanted. They said, "You can sell anything if you price it low enough."

> *I got full price and all the terms we wanted. I didn't see that I was doing anything wrong. There was a waiting line outside, we had numerous showings, Bob's house sold in less than a week, and he was fishing in upstate NY in the summer of 1990 because that was all he wanted.*

The listing presentation — your time to shine

If you were going for a job interview, you would find out everything you could about the position and the company first, wouldn't you? A listing appointment is just that — you interviewing for the job of agent. You want to prepare by investing the time in learning as much as you can before you are sitting face-to-face with the sellers. The secret to a successful listing is the information you gather *prior to the listing*.

- Why are you selling and moving?
- When do you need to move?
- How much do you think the house will sell for?
- How much do you need from the sale? I take that figure and add closing costs plus commission and some wiggle room. Then I write the number down in my file on separate paper and say, "You do not have to sign a contract that will not clear this amount."
- Prepare the seller by saying, "Here is what we need: a copy of the deed, copy of the plat, copy of your title policy, your payoff information, the code for the security system if there is one, and a key for me." (If the key is there when you arrive, consider the listing yours!)
- Will everyone who is on the title be there for the listing appointment? If not, you could be wasting your time. Do you need a power of attorney? Do you need a death certificate? Proof of ground rent or fee simple?

Do your homework; have comps, actives, solds, pendings, sold without an agent. (If something's been on the market for months, I don't call them "actives," I call them "properties that are not selling.")

When you're ready to meet with the sellers, go in to the appointment knowing that you can afford not to get the listing. No matter how big the listing, no matter how important the sellers could be to your career, *you do not need the listing.* Be ready to walk away without hesitation. That attitude gives you incredible power, and it shows. It's not arrogance, it's just the calm confidence that people want to be associated with.

Most listing presentations are formal, but some can be as simple as a casual conversation. When you are prepared to talk real estate anytime, anywhere, you might find yourself going from conversation to listing in minutes. My second listing was like that.

A friend of mine had a small home she needed to sell and had already tried the do-it-yourself route. She ran ads in the paper and put up flyers in her neighborhood, but no one had been to look at it. This was back in the dark ages before the Internet and Websites changed the world of real estate, so her choices for getting the word out were limited.

One day she told me what she was doing and that she'd offer me the listing but couldn't afford to use a real estate agent. I said, "You can't afford NOT to use me!" It took some convincing, but once I explained that my commission would come out of the extra I would sell the house for — making sure she got the amount she needed — she agreed.

Where I got the nerve back then, on only my second listing, I don't know, but I priced the property well above what she was asking on her own. And after only a couple of showings, we had a full-price contract!

> *One of the nicest results is that these sellers, skeptical in the beginning, become some of your best sources of referrals. And sometimes, good friends, too.*

There's a common real estate term that a lot of people in the industry would say applies to that second listing: "FSBO" ("For Sale by Owner"). But I don't use that term because I don't think of them as selling their homes, I think of them as unrepresented sellers.

Over time, I've changed my listing presentation, but there are three essential questions that are always part of the discussion:

1. **Are you sure you want to sell?** This one is critical, and why you need all parties (usually a couple) there at the same time. Too often I've seen one say "Absolutely!" while the other hesitates, won't make eye contact, and either say nothing or say "Yes" while the body language is screaming "No!" When this happens, take time to talk it through. If they don't both really agree, you may get the listing, but never get to the settlement table.
2. **Do you have any questions about my company?** Usually the answer is "No," because they are listing with me, not the company. Of course, if your broker is a well-known name either locally or nationally, that won't hurt.
3. **Are you 100% sure you want to use me?** This is the most important of the three. Until you have a "Yes" on this, don't even discuss the commission; if you don't get the listing, your commission rate could be used against you by the next agent in.

Why should I list with you?
You are in a listing presentation, it's going well, and then the prospect asks that eternal question: "Why should I use you?" How do you answer? That depends on where you are in your career.

As a rookie, you can say what I told Bob: "I know that my career depends on selling your home and doing it right. I have the training and support, and my company wants me to be successful, which means they will help me do a great job for you. You have the advantage of my full attention. All my energy and advertising will be for your benefit." Let your earnestness and enthusiasm come through; people love to help someone who is trying to learn and grow.

Further down the road, with more sales under your belt, you can point to your experience and knowledge of the market. If you have specialized in one area, you can say, "I know this neighborhood well and can help buyers see the advantage of your house over any others in the area."

One thing that worked for me as my career grew was my Brag Book (also called a "portable wall") that I took on listing appointments. In it I put the flyers from other listings, thank you notes from happy clients, certifications for continuing education, everything I could think of that showed how I do business. I would let people look through the book while I measured their home, helping confirm the decision they just made to list with me.

No matter where you are in your career, there's a good answer to "Why should I list with you?" After a few years, with dozens of sales to your credit and a good referral base, you will find that the conversation changes. Instead of "Why should I use you?" the question you will hear is "Will you please list our house?" That's confirmation that you are doing real estate the right way.

Setting the price and dealing with the "C" word

You've done your homework so you know what similar homes have sold for in the area. You have read the comps and compared them with the house you are listing. But all that is not as important as what the sellers want and need to get from the sale — and "want" and "need" are not always the same. They want to get the most they can. So do you. But what you need to know is their bottom line. What is the balance on their mortgage, and is there a second mortgage or line of credit that also has to be paid off?

To a large extent the market will set the price, but you need to know what price will clear what they need plus closing costs and commissions. If what they can reasonably get for the house is less than they need, maybe they can't actually afford to sell right now and should wait for a better market or pay down their loans some more. Obviously, you want to find this out as quickly as possible so you don't waste your time or theirs.

But, if you're able to agree on a price that they will accept and at which you think you can sell the house, it's time to deal with the "C" word. In that first listing I didn't mention commission because I didn't know I "should" and because Bob didn't ask. But most people will, so you need to be ready.

When talking with a seller, whether they've tried to sell on their own or not, I always ask one important question: "You tell me what you need from the sale, your bottom line; if I can get that for you, what difference does my commission make?" The answer is, of course, that *the commission is not really the issue.* What matters is that the sellers receive the payout they want and need.

Choosing to negotiate the commission rate is a decision you'll have to make for yourself. Today there are multiple business models to choose from in real estate; they run the gamut from full-service commission, to discounting, to auction where the seller pays no commission, to professional consulting with the ACRE™ (Accredited Consultant in Real Estate) designation, where you charge for specific services up front. Whatever your choice, keep in mind that you are negotiating your worth, and if you don't believe you are worth a full-service commission or a professional consulting fee, then you might want to step back and look at your choice of real estate as a career. Again, it's not arrogance, but confidence and knowing the value of the service you offer your clients.

There's a rampant belief that getting an agent to agree to a lower commission is always good for the seller. Why agree to a full-service commission if you can talk them down to a lower commission? After all, if the agent gets less, that means the seller gets more, right? Not necessarily!

What does a seller really want? To sell their house for the best possible price and keep as much of the sales price as possible. That's obvious. But how do you get the best possible price? By getting as many agents as possible to show and promote your house. And what makes an agent want to show your house? A fair commission. So, if you were an agent and one listing promised you a higher commission and another promised substantially less, which one would you take your buyers to? Right — the one with the higher commission.

That makes sense for the Realtor®, but what about the seller? Here's another story that says it all:

> *A client of mine decided to sell his home without agent representation. His wife wanted me as their agent, but he was determined to do it on his own. Not surprisingly, nothing happened. Realtor®s have only so much time to show potential buyers the available houses, and they aren't going to send someone to a for-sale-by-owner that has no commission attached.*
>
> *After a while with no action, the husband decided to take on an agent, a low-cost one. He bargained hard and got a rock-bottom commission rate. And again, nothing happened; no sign, no advertising, no calls, and no showings. Finally, as their anniversary approached, his wife put her foot down. For her anniversary gift she wanted just one thing: "I*

> *want to sell my home with Margaret Rome." Reluctantly, he agreed.*
>
> *And then things started to happen. We talked about what they wanted to net out of the property, then we listed it at a price higher than that used by the low cost agent and with a full-service commission. Within the very first week, we had a full-price contract. The house that wouldn't sell as a FSBO or as a reduced-service commission suddenly became attractive to other real estate agents and the buyers they brought with them.*
>
> *Like they say, you really do get what you pay for!*

There's a long-term benefit to valuing yourself and your service right. You become known as an agent who delivers and who treats everyone fairly. Referrals — the best kind of business — come from the people who sign a full-commission agreement and see their house sell for what you all agreed was the right price. They send you new clients, and your reputation grows.

It really does work, no matter what the market. But if you're still tempted to discount your way to the bottom just to get a listing, keep this story in mind. I call it "The Five Dollar Haircut."

> *Once upon a time there was a thriving upscale hair salon. Businessmen, businesswomen, and society people from all over came to have their hair styled and cut.*
>
> *But then a big chain of discount hair cutters came into town. They advertised $5 haircuts. Their signs were everywhere. They had billboards. They advertised on radio and on TV. And they were doing a tremendous amount of business with $5 haircuts.*
>
> *The operators at The Salon were losing customers. They went to the owner and said, "We have to reduce our prices.*

> We cannot compete. We are surrounded by these $5 haircut people!"
>
> The owner just smiled a wise smile and assured them he had a solution. He knew that his salon was first class, that his stylists were the best, and that reducing his fees was not the answer. He had another plan.
>
> The next morning when the operators came to work they saw this small sign in front of The Salon:
>
> ### WE FIX $5 HAIRCUTS

There will always be someone willing to discount their value to get business. You get to choose whether you want to be the one who does $5 haircuts or the Fifth Avenue Salon with the waiting list for $100 haircuts.

While we're talking about long-term benefits, sometimes you are better off *not* making a deal if you sense that your seller or buyer is compromising too much for their own good. One of the important features you offer as a professional Realtor® is an un-emotional viewpoint.

> We've all had this happen. We work with someone for a while, showing them houses that we think are right, or that they want to see. One day they say, "This is the one — I want this house."
>
> Instead of whipping out a contract offer and saying "Sign here," try asking a few questions first. I did this recently and helped someone avoid what could have been a mistake. But I didn't tell her; she came to the conclusion on her own.
>
> I asked, "What do you like so much about this house?" She answered with the obvious things — the land around it, the building that would house her office, a wonderful updated kitchen. Those are the tangibles, the things that are easy to

identify. It's the intangibles, though, that make a home. It's the intangibles that make you feel safe, happy, and relaxed when you walk into the right home. Or uneasy, annoyed, and ill at ease when it's not quite right.

In this case, the house was older and had small rooms and low ceilings; she and her husband were moving from a newer home with high ceilings. When I asked how she would feel walking into the master bedroom, her first response was about the low ceilings.

Before long the rosy picture she had painted for herself — she really wanted to like this house — began to change in the light of reality. We didn't make an offer on that house. I passed up a sale that day, and solidified a relationship that will continue for years beyond this one transaction.

· · · · ·

When I was in nursing I learned a lot about human behavior and psychology; nurses have to read nonverbal signals to help them understand their patient's needs. Realtors® aren't therapists, but we need a lot of those same skills to understand our client's needs. It's not difficult; watch, ask questions, and then listen.

There are many ways to sell houses. How well you are able to see or create opportunities can make a big difference in the level of your success. It's important to know how to read the nonverbal signals people send. There's a book called *Signals: What Your Child Is Really Telling You* written by Murray Kappleman and Paul Ackerman. Murray was the Chief of Pediatrics at Sinai Hospital in Baltimore when I was Chief Pediatric Nurse. He wrote about understanding the signals the patients are giving you. I learned a lot from Murray, and later saw a very practical demonstration of the importance of taking the time to listen carefully to all the signals, not just the verbal ones.

> *When my daughter Erica was seven years old, she was already playing the piano and showing great ability. The Peabody Institute came to test her for piano talent at her school; I was not there for the testing but was sure of my daughter's ability. You can imagine my surprise when they reported that Erica "has extreme talent but she hates the instrument." I thought they had to be wrong. We could hardly keep Erica away from the piano; we even had to use playing the piano as a reward!*
>
> *Erica quit taking lessons after that. But when I finally asked why she told the man from Peabody that she hated the piano, the truth made seven-year-old sense: She didn't want him to be her teacher. Thank goodness we asked! Erica became a successful professional pianist and accompanist.*

Remember that not every message is verbal or written. In fact, it's well-known that tone and body language carry much of the message, so watch and listen. You'll gather valuable understanding that will help you work with and for your clients.

What about unrepresented sellers?

Can you really convert them to listings? Yes, armed with the right information. People believe that they will save money by selling their house without using a Realtor®. Research has shown, though, that in 2007 the typical unrepresented seller's home sold for $187,200, compared to $247,000 for agent-assisted home sales.[1] That's a difference of $59,800. Even if each of those homes had a 6 percent commission, the net difference in sale price would be more than $56,000!

---

1 National Association of REALTORS®, 2007 NAR Profile of Home Buyers and Sellers.

Price is what people think of first when they think about selling their home, but it's not the only issue. Sellers who try to go it alone are usually unprepared for the complexity of the paperwork that is part of today's house sale. Worse, they don't know where the traps are that a knowledgeable agent could help them avoid. We hear stories all the time about sales that fall through leaving the do-it-yourself seller with a contract that didn't get to settlement. Too often, they've already moved and are left saddled with two mortgages.

No matter what the market, anyone can sell a house. Put a "For Sale" sign out front and eventually you'll probably get offers. What a Realtor® does is not just help sell the house; the Realtor® makes sure the client gets from sale to settlement. That's where the real work is done.

What do I mean by "real work"? That's up next, in Chapter 5.

CHAPTER FOUR – LISTING, LISTING, WHO'S GOT THE LISTING?
☐ Prepare for your listing appointments by asking questions and learning as much as you can about the sellers and their needs.
☐ Be ready to answer "Why should I list with you?" and "Will you discount your commission?"
☐ Approach each potential listing knowing that you don't need to get it.

FIVE
YOU GOT THE LISTING...
NOW WHAT?

That new listing is glowing in your hands, full of promise and possibility. What do you do now to turn it into a successful sale and a happy client at the settlement table? It certainly takes more than those infamous Three Ps:

1. Put it in the multiple list
2. Put a sign in the ground
3. Pray!

There are dozens of ways to draw agents and buyers to your property, hundreds of places to advertise, scores of techniques that improve the attractiveness of the house. What do you do first?

Obviously, you do those first two Ps — make sure your signs are on the property, and that it is entered in the multiple list correctly. You choose for yourself about that third P.

One of the first things I do is give the sellers a list of repairs they need to make along with suggestions for touching up, adding curb appeal, decluttering, and staging if I think it will make a difference. Making the house salable is the sellers' primary responsibility, and there is always too much inventory to spend my advertising dollars and time on a property that is not salable. Even when working with sellers who have been clients before, I remind them that I have to sell the house three times: once to other agents so they will bring potential buyers, a second time to the buyers, and a third time to the appraiser and sometimes the underwriter. This helps them understand the importance of presenting the house in its best light, and at the same time reinforces the value of working with a professional Realtor®.

List 'em, they will come

When the home is ready to show, how do you get buyers to the door? You'll recall from the first chapter that advertising is one of the basic costs of being a professional real estate agent. Just as you advertise to build your brand and avoid being a "secret agent," so you advertise to let the world know about this fantastic property you've just listed. And you don't do this in only one place, and not just one time. On your first few listings, you need to be ready to make the investment, even before the first transaction closes and you get that first commission check.

Why is advertising so important? After all, the property is in the multiple list and all the other brokers and agents can find it there, right? Uh-huh, right there along with all the thousands of other properties vying for attention. If you blend in with the surroundings, how can you expect to be seen?

A few years ago I had one of those "Ah ha!" moments about how and why advertising is for the birds.

> *While visiting our friend and neighbor a couple of doors away, I noticed her tiny aviary — a couple of bird feeders and a birdbath. It was the end of May, and the area was filled with the fluttering of colorful singers.*

It looked like a nice little hobby and I have the perfect spot…a big tree near my front porch and rocking chairs. I decided to get a feeder and found there were so many decisions: what type of feeder, what kind of birds do you want, what type of food, what type of stand or hanger?

I started with one bird feeder. It was tubular, used thistle, and attracted smaller varieties like the pretty little yellow finches. Well, I waited for over a month. The feeder was still full and no birds were eating my thistle, even though I knew they were just a few houses away.

Did I say, "Forget about it," and leave the birds to find other food? Nope. I went out and bought another bird feeder, this time one that would attract larger birds. And, of course, this one required a different type of feed, mostly sunflower seeds. Oh, and then I needed a container for the feed, and special hooks for the feeder, etc.

We set it all up and attracted…squirrels. Should I have gotten the one that flips these rodents off? No, they need to eat, and they are great acrobats to watch, but they were keeping the birds away. So then I switched the two feeders, placing the small one closer to the tree and the large one that the squirrels liked farther out where they couldn't get to it.

Success! Within a few days we had birds — goldfinches, wrens, cardinals, and others that I have not even tried to identify. In a matter of a day and a half the feeders went from full to half-gone. Yep, it was working.

It's just like advertising. You have to make decisions; what type of ad, what publication, which type size, and which location in the publication. The phone almost never rings with a first ad. It takes time, it takes tweaking, it takes knowing who your audience is and where they are. You have to keep the feeder filled.

> *I created an ad for a specific type of buyer, like setting out thistle seed to bring goldfinches to my yard. I could have stopped advertising after the first month when nothing happened and said, "Ads just don't work." I could have removed the ad from that publication. Instead, I chose to place another ad in a different publication looking for a broader type of buyer — just like adding a large feeder with different type of seed to attract larger birds, and a copper birdbath that hangs from the tree.*
>
> *The phone started ringing, and the birds flocked around. Now there is a dove that competes with the squirrels for the seeds that drop to the ground. More choices, broader advertising, and I have more diversity of "customers" in my little aviary. There's even a black cat that sees it as a private entertainment center for her and her kittens — a bit more diversity than I aimed for, but you don't always get what you expect from advertising either!*

Where and how you advertise will depend on your market. In some places it's all print, and in others everything is online, and others it's a mix. When you're new to real estate, study what other agents and brokers are doing. Talk to people in your office about what works for them. Go online and join a real estate focused group like Active Rain (read more about this later in Chapter 9.) When you talk with prospective buyers and sellers, ask where they saw your ad and where they go to find out about properties for sale. Ask questions, listen to the answers, and choose what works for you and your market.

It's time for show and sell
From Chapter 2, you already know that I make my own appointments and why. It is one of the basics of controlling the quality of

service my clients receive. But I also do my own showings as often as possible. This is something that's been discussed a lot in some of the online real estate groups, and some people seem to think that a listing agent who wants to be there for a showing gets in the way of making a sale. Worse, some buyer's agents are afraid that the listing agent is trying to steal their client.

I absolutely disagree. It's not that I don't have enough to fill up my time. And no, I'm not a greedy listing agent wanting to steal buyers; I have all the referrals I can handle and then some. What I do want is to *get the house sold!*

It all comes down to the level of service that I want for my clients. I choose to limit my clients to special people, people I really want to work with. Taking care of sellers is the most important thing I do, and that means I make the appointments and, if at all possible, I do the showings. I've had many sellers who wanted and needed me to be there during a showing: elderly people, recent widows and widowers, young families with small children, people with pets, and those with other special needs.

Anyone can put on a lock box, put up a sign, set a low price, and then wait for the contracts. I choose to go for quality first, and that means that having a lot of people traipsing through is not necessarily the best way to sell a house. Ask yourself: If you were showing your parents' home, would you want a lock box and uncontrolled showings? Or would you like an agent you trust to be looking out for Mom and Dad?

Selling a home is stressful. Showings are stressful. My job is to do whatever I can to alleviate the stress for my sellers, and to share the frustration when an agent is two hours late or does not show up or call. To allay the stress when an agent shows up but doesn't come in. I am *not* there to make it easy for agents who are not prepared or who make a bunch of appointments on the spur of the moment.

I explain all this to my sellers. We may have fewer showings — we may even miss an occasional showing. But the buyers and agents who call about the home will talk with me to make the appointments, and then I have an opportunity to share special things about the property. Yes, all the information about the property is in the listing, but not every agent reads past the price and address before taking their buyer out. And some are not aware of the importance of specifics about the property that I can explain. For example, I saved countless hours by not showing a particular property with what looked like a terrific price, because people read "co-op" and thought it meant "condo." But it's not the same. This co-op requires cash contracts only, so there can be no mortgage, and it does not allow pets.

By talking with prospective buyers or their agents first, I could save everyone a lot of time while saving my clients the extra stress of having showings that should never have happened.

I always tell the agents if I will be there for the showing, and always ask if they have a problem with my presence. I have found that 99 percent of them appreciate my being there to point out features of the home, especially if they have never seen the property. Then I go into another room and allow them to stay as long as they like while I do other work. But if they don't want me there, they can say so.

Recently I met an agent at one of my new listings. The first thing he said was, "This is just too small. There's no way they will have any interest."

He was not even going to let his buyers come in. I asked that since they were already there, would they please come in and take a look around? Then I had the opportunity to say, "Yes, it is a small house. But did you see the family room which can be a third bedroom or guest room? And did you see the size of the yard and the hot tub? Did you notice the pull-down stairs with access to attic storage?" The buyers fell in love with the house and wound up writing an over list, non-contingent contract with a quick settlement.

At first the agent was not happy with me, but now he sings my praises for the helpful information I was able to give him and his buyers. He also got a bit of education in the process. He had never heard of a house built on a slab, had never heard of radiant heat. He was very grateful to have me share this information and help "close" his buyers so he could get a commission.

It does not matter whether the listing is a million dollar mansion or a fixer-upper row house. I'm there for the showings, and yes, it does make a difference.

We're having an open house!

Is there anything that says "Real Estate" louder than those "Open!" signs that spring up on the weekends with arrows pointing in every direction? Open houses are a tradition in selling homes, but not for me.

Because I believe in the personal approach to selling — focusing on finding the best qualified buyers for my listings — I have never found that the traditional approach of open houses gives a good return on my investment of time and advertising money. But of course there are exceptions. Sometimes you will have a property that is so different, such a challenge to sell, that you have to be creative and try something different like a barbecue open house.

Remember we said that creative problem-solving is an important skill for real estate agents? The "unsalable" house will have you thinking way outside that box to come up with attention-getting events. Here's a good example:

A couple of years ago I had the opportunity to take on a unique, "impossible" listing. These are so much fun because they have been on the market for a while and haven't sold. Nothing gets my creative juices flowing faster than a challenge that "can't be done."

At first glance it was a lovely old country church complete with steeple and stained glass. A second look revealed a modern section attached to one side with lots of windows angled to capture the sun.

Stepping inside you found yourself in a soaring space that held an art gallery as well as the artist's home and studio. Natural light poured in all around you, and the white walls made a perfect setting for the imagination to roam free.

I could see this used as a gallery, as it was then, but also as studio space for artists and craftsmen, a graphic design studio, an architect's office, even home to someone's collection of antique dolls or a grand model railroad garden. With livable space inside and out, the possibilities were literally endless!

Sure, it was not for everyone, but for the right person or group, this wonderful building could have been the perfect answer to their dreams.

The seller was a ceramic artist and multi-talented creative spirit. She had been there for 30 years and provided documents on the history of the building that we used in the advertising and marketing.

We used many avenues to draw attention to the property, including a contest to come up with the most creative use for the space, discussion of the home on a weekly radio show, and yes, an open house. But it was not your everyday open house.

The evening was a hot one, even for early September in the Baltimore area. There was already a crowd gathering outside, but to be fair to the owners, we wouldn't open until the official start time. After all, it's not easy getting 6,000 sq.ft. in open house condition, while working full-time, having a life, and sharing the space with a couple of beautiful greyhounds.

Before the opening I had time to talk with the crowd of more than 30 prospective buyers and share all the wonderful stuff I knew about this historic building and the artist, Tatiana. I showed them the cornerstone that reads 1889, and we had time to walk the property and see the freestanding building that housed Tatiana's kiln. The building would make a great workshop, classroom, or storage space.

The adjacent cemetery brought different reactions from people. The cemetery was established when the building was used as a church, and was sold many years ago to the former congregation who still care for it. Some people — often the creative artists and writers — found the space very calming and peaceful. The extensive decking provided the perfect place to sit and contemplate.

There were plenty of questions and it was great to watch the anticipation build as the time grew close to go inside. Not everything about the building is clear from the outside, and the green-house windows drew plenty of speculation. Designed by Tatiana's late husband, who was an architect and used it as his studio, this part of the addition had its own private front entrance as well as a "secret" curved stairway to the inside of the house.

When the doors opened at 6:30, it was fun to watch the expressions of young and old take in the huge space with the original ceilings, floors, and windows. And then to see how

> *Tatiana made use of the gourmet kitchen and the huge sunroom.*
>
> *I asked the children if they would like to live here, and was answered with such excitement, "Yeah, this would be cool!" So I suggested they all go pick out their rooms and then report back to me. One wanted the studio apartment, one wanted the cool room upstairs with the round stained window, one wanted Tatiana's bedroom and was fascinated by her bright red Japanese soaking tub. Remember, I was using my former pediatric R.N. training — get the kids involved.*
>
> *I pointed out the possibility of using the huge library as a master bedroom since it has a full bath attached. The glaze-room area with its small office and bath would be an ideal place for a laundry. And that still left four bedrooms plus two more baths and a full laundry upstairs.*
>
> *We stayed until almost 9:00 p.m., sitting outside and talking about how successful the open house was and what good energy we all felt. With champagne and popcorn, this was definitely not your everyday open house!*

Whether you choose to have open houses will depend on the traditions in your market, as well as on how you structure your own real estate practice. For me, open houses are the exception rather than the rule because the investment of time and money rarely pays off better than taking the more personal approach.

And you'll see more of that ahead in Chapter 6, where you'll learn a new four-letter word that is sure to become your new favorite!

CHAPTER FIVE – YOU GOT THE LISTING...NOW WHAT?
☐ Making the home salable is your sellers' responsibility, and you can help by suggesting how to make it more attractive to other agents, buyers, and appraisers.
☐ Whether you choose print or online or even skywriting, you must invest in advertising to build your business and sell your listings; don't be a secret agent!
☐ Attend as many showings as you can for your listings; your knowledge of the home's features can help the buyers' agent make the sale.
☐ Exercise your creativity to draw attention to an open house.

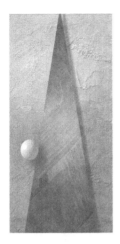

SIX
LET'S MAKE A DEAL

There's an old saying in real estate: "Houses sell houses. Agents screw up deals." And all too often this is true. As agents we can get so involved in trying to make a deal go through that we don't slow down enough to listen to what our sellers and buyers are telling us. I believe there is a buyer for every house, but just like finding your one true love, you may have to wait awhile for that buyer to be in the right place at the right time to meet the house you are selling. As Realtors®, it's just good practice to discuss the various options to potential buyers based on our experience. But as professionals we also have to know when to shut up and let the house speak to the buyer. The entire purpose of this chapter is to help you make a good deal, and to help the houses sell.

Choosing your buyers and sellers

Choosing? Don't I mean finding and signing buyers and sellers? That's important, of course, but choosing who you want to work with comes first. When we are new agents, we tend to grab anyone who is willing to sign with us, and that's understandable — we need experience and the only way to get it is to, well, get it. But before you slip that listing under your seller's pen, pause for a moment and ask yourself:

- **Will this seller accept some advice on showing the home?** If someone resists when you suggest decluttering, basic maintenance, and touch up, your job will be more difficult and the house will not sell as well.
- **Are these sellers fully committed to selling their home now?** This is essential. Especially if the market is not strong, someone who just wants to "see what I can get" won't be motivated to accept a decent offer, and you may be wasting your time.
- **Does the seller understand completely how we arrived at the selling price,** and is willing to adjust the price later, if necessary? Even the most reasonable home owners can become a bit greedy when they start to imagine how much they might get for their home. Once the asking price is set, people start to feel that they are *entitled* to that price, and resist a suggestion to reduce it later on. When you start off with a high price and then reduce it, the sellers think they have "lost" that amount, even though they didn't have it at the right price to begin with.
- **Will this seller call me ten times a day for updates,** even when I've already reported any current activity? You have to establish the sellers' needs and how you communicate with them. Some people want a daily update, and some only want to hear from you when you have a contract in hand. But the important thing is to establish expectations. When do they want to be called? What time? How often? One client got up at 5:30 a.m. with her dogs and wanted me to call her then

— that was OK, she was on West Coast time — while another didn't get up until 10:30. You lose more clients by lack of communication than any other means — they want to know you haven't forgotten them.

- **Will the sellers negotiate any of the contract terms when a good buyer appears?** It's not unusual to have some additional terms in a contract. Appliances and window treatments are typical, but you might also find that including a particular piece of furniture can make a deal go through. I find out up front what's really important to the seller — what can go and what absolutely has to stay — and make note of it. Then when a buyer comes in and loves the fixture, I say, "Let me see if I can get that for you." That makes the buyer feel more special. But you have to know what's excluded.

> *Many years ago I listed a log cabin home in the woods, a home that needed a very special buyer. It was the first log home that I ever listed and thought it would be impossible to sell; boy, was I wrong! I had more calls on that property than any other. One day another agent brought a young family to look at the property, and I noticed that the kids were having such a good time with the owner's dog.*
>
> *Knowing that my seller was moving out of the country, I asked about his pet. He was concerned; the puppy had never known another home, and to transport him would not be easy. I suggested writing the dog into the contract. It was the first time that a dog was a part of one of my transactions, but that is what helped make it work.*

- **Do I understand what is important to the sellers?** Have I asked enough questions and learned enough about them to know why they are selling, why now, and what they need from the sale in both money and time to settlement? Most importantly, do I understand the various emotional issues that can be part of the undercurrent in any deal, like that seller's concern for his dog? All of this is important for a good deal.

- **Am I competent to take this listing and do a good job for the seller?** Of course you know the rules and regulations of real estate — that's not the question. But if you've spent all your career specializing in one area, and you have the chance to list a home in the historic preservation district that is in the process of being rehabbed, do you know the issues you might face? Can you guide a buyer through the regulations that apply in these special circumstances? Do you know reliable resources for the kind of work they will need to finish the job? I'm not saying don't take the listing or buyer's agency, but rather that you be sure you can give the buyer or seller what they need. Perhaps you can work with an experienced agent or hire a consultant to fill in the gaps until you learn.

- **Do I like these sellers? Can I work with them?** You're not required to be a friend to your clients, but you do need to like them enough to go through several months or more of close communication during a very stressful period in their lives. If you don't at least feel they can be trusted, if you don't believe they will work with you cooperatively, then don't sign the contract. Remember, you are not losing an opportunity — you are making room for a better client and a better deal.

Getting ready to sell

We talked in Chapter 5 about getting the house ready to show and sell. But there's another way you can help your sellers get ready for a sale — by getting their paperwork in order ahead of time. Anyone who has bought, sold, or refinanced a house in the last few years knows that there are massive stacks of papers that have to be signed before the keys change hands. Fortunately for the buyers and sellers, most of those papers come from the Realtor®, the title company, and the lender.

But even before the first offer comes in, sellers should be finding the "other" paperwork. Those are the papers that — depending on how long they've been in the home — might be scattered or buried in old files or boxes:

1. The settlement documents from when they bought the house; these would include the contract, the settlement sheet, loan documents, title insurance, plats, easements, ground rents, and any others that they received at settlement.

2. Any other loan documents from a refinancing, home equity line of credit, or second mortgage, along with the loan numbers and bank information.

3. Receipts and permits for any major improvements or renovations such as adding a bathroom or extending a deck.

4. Warranty information for any appliances or home systems that have been added, repaired, or replaced recently.

5. Homeowner association, condo, or co-op documents, including any documents that show they have complied with the rules for renovations or additions such as decks or color changes.

6. Tax receipts and bills that will show a prospective buyer what the gas, electric, water, and tax charges have been for the past year.

Having these ready before you list and sell the home will help things run more smoothly. And when the house is sold, and they pack those papers to move, remind your sellers to keep the first three on the list together with the new settlement papers — they will need them again come April for tax time.

Agents and brokers and others

One of the great pleasures — and sometimes the great pains — of real estate is working with other agents and brokers. There are wonderful people in this profession, people who give their time and talent to help others, people who go out of their way to mentor new agents, people who look after their clients with the care and protective instincts of a mother bear. These are the agents you meet over a transaction and look for ways to work together again. They are the ones you send referrals to when you can't or don't want to handle a particular client. They are golden, and you treasure them as colleagues and friends.

And there is the other kind, which I hope you rarely meet. You will sometimes have to work with agents you do not respect, who are unreliable or unresponsive, or whose ethics are a bit too flexible. When you run into one of these, the best thing you can do is take the high road.

I remember in my first Fast Start class at what was then O'Conor, Piper & Flynn in Baltimore, the president of the company, Bill Flynn, told us, "If there's a question about ethics, walk away." We live and prosper on our reputations, and nothing will trash your reputation faster than being involved in an unethical transaction. How can you be sure if what you see is unethical?

Your answer is in the question! If your gut is not happy with the situation, if your B.S. detector is sounding the alarm, if your nose smells something fishy, well, there it is. Run, do not walk, away from that situation.

That takes care of the clearly unethical situation, but what if it's not a question of ethics, just that the other agent is kindness-impaired. It's true, sometimes you really won't like or respect the agent on the other side of the transaction, but you can still make the deal work. Figure out a way to make that person like and respect you:

- Do everything you can to keep relations cordial, or at the very least civil. This can make the difference between a smooth and a horrible transaction.
- Keep an even temper and tone in all your dealings. Even if they're screaming at you, keep your voice low and your tone reasonable. (Of course, you don't have to put up with profanity or abuse.) Use any tricks you need to resist yelling back or telling them off. Picture your clients happy at the end of the transaction — that's what you're working for.
- Remember that success is the best revenge!

There are many other professionals you'll work with between contract signing and settlement. Inspectors, appraisers, lenders, and others have an influence on how quickly and easily you will get to the table.

Real Estate Appraisers. Your mortgage lender will require an appraisal of the home to verify that the property has a market value of at least the amount being requested by the buyer. Even though you could argue the market price is what the house sold for, the lender needs an independent authority to verify the value. Appraisers are licensed by the state in which they operate, and are expected to be an objective party with no connection to anyone involved in the transaction.

In years when the market price of homes was rising rapidly, we sometimes found that a home would not appraise for the agreed-upon selling price. That's when your skills as a real estate agent may make the difference between a deal that goes through and one that dies at the appraisal stage.

Appraisers are human, too. They generally appreciate the kind of help you can give them that doesn't try to influence the outcome of their appraisal. For instance:

- Don't let the appraiser go in alone — be there so that you can answer questions and see the process.
- Have a copy of the plat for the appraiser along with a plan of the house and room measurements. You are saving the appraiser time by providing factual information.
- Have copies of your comps to give the appraiser. Make sure you have found the right comps, not just the first ones that might come up when the appraiser does a search. More than once I've been able to support the sale price by checking properties that have sold through agents and those not listed by using the tax records to see properties that have transferred without an agent.

Lenders. Building a good working relationship with more than one lender, whether a bank or a mortgage company, helps your clients and your business. This is another area where reputation matters and where people in the community learn quickly who is good to deal with. As a real estate agent, you will have many lenders wanting you to send them qualified clients.

I tell buyers, "I sell houses, lenders sell money. If you can convince a lender or broker to give you the money, I will then show you any house. I really don't care how much you make, how much you owe, or how many times you've been bankrupt."

Home Inspectors. I feel very strongly about this: Whether your client is the seller or buyer, you *must* be present for the home inspection. An inspector's report can read like the house is about to fall down or like the house is perfection in every way; neither is likely to be true. Many deals that I have seen fall apart are because of the home inspection report.

A good home inspection will take several hours, and done right, it can be like having a group meeting. It gives me a chance to get my team together — appraiser, termite inspector, lender. I find the home inspection time more productive than any open house. In a window of a few hours, I can get trades there to look at any issues and advise on cost or stability of the issue. This saves a great deal of time.

- During the inspection, be sure you understand what the inspector finds, and ask for an explanation if you don't.
- Do not buy into any statements that indicate catastrophe; ask for a detailed explanation of the cause and effect of the apparent defect. If you can't see what the inspector is talking about, consider having a specialist in that area (roofing, foundation, etc.) look at it and give you a second opinion.
- When a repair is indicated, ask the inspector, "If this were yours, how would you fix it?" The answer may lead to a simpler solution or to a change in your contract terms.

Home inspection is one of the more stressful events between contract and settlement. For your peace of mind and that of your client, watch, listen, and learn all you can during it.

Title Companies. Title companies provide title insurance services to buyers, sellers, and lenders by performing a title search to determine if the seller has the legal right to sell the property. The search also verifies the status of property taxes, determines whether there are any liens against the property, and prepares the Settlement Statement. During the settlement, which often takes place at the company's office, the title company is responsible for collecting and disbursing the monies that change hands.

My preference is that either I know the lender or the title company, or that the lender and title company know each other. This helps to reduce finger pointing if there are any glitches with paperwork or getting everything together for the settlement. I do try to discourage people from using one of the many Internet lenders who survive on volume; to them, if a deal falls through, it's no big deal. But it's a very big deal to my client.

Making sure of a clear title often is a simple matter. But then there are properties with a long history. Whether the following story[1] is absolutely true or not, we can all relate to the unique challenges that bureaucracies present us with.

A New Orleans lawyer sought an FHA loan for a client who lost his house in Hurricane Katrina and wanted to rebuild. He was told the loan would be granted if he could prove satisfactory title to the parcel of property being offered as collateral. The title to the property dated back to 1803, which took the lawyer three months to track down. After sending the information to the FHA, he received the following reply:

1 Reprinted from a widely circulated email, author unknown.

"Upon review of your letter adjoining your client's loan application, we note that the request is supported by an Abstract of Title. While we compliment the able manner in which you have prepared and presented the application, we must point out that you have only cleared title to the proposed collateral property back to 1803. Before final approval can be accorded, it will be necessary to clear the title back to its origin."

Annoyed, the lawyer responded as follows:

"Your letter regarding title in Case No. 189156 has been received. I note that you wish to have title extended further than the 194 years covered by the present application. I was unaware that any educated person in this country, particularly those working in the property area, would not know that Louisiana was purchased, by the U.S., from France in 1803, the year of origin identified in our application.

"For the edification of uninformed FHA bureaucrats, the title to the land prior to U.S. ownership was obtained from France, which had acquired it by Right of Conquest from Spain. The land came into the possession of Spain by Right of Discovery made in the year 1492 by a sea captain named Christopher Columbus, who had been granted the privilege of seeking a new route to India by the Spanish monarch, Isabella.

"The good queen Isabella, being a pious woman and almost as careful about titles as the FHA, took the precaution of securing the blessing of the Pope before she sold her jewels to finance Columbus' expedition. Now the Pope, as I'm sure you may know, is the emissary of the Son of God, and God, it is commonly accepted, created this world. Therefore, I believe it is safe to presume that God also made that part of the world called Louisiana. God, therefore, would be the owner

> *of origin and His origins date back to before the beginning of time, the world as we know it AND the FHA.*
>
> *I hope you find God's original claim to be satisfactory. Now, may we have our damn loan?"*
>
> *He got the loan.*

The Trades. Unless the home you've just listed is brand new, it probably needs some fixing up before you open it to potential buyers. Remember my first sale (Chapter 4) and how I told Bob that he had to replace that orange shag carpet? The name I gave him was someone who had done work in my home. And that's how you start — with people who you have worked with for your own home, or whose work you have seen.

The longer you are in the business, the longer your list will be of companies and individuals you can call for quick service, quality work, and fair pricing. Over time, you will have a roofer, painter, carpet company, stager, decorator, termite and pest control service, locksmith, plumber, electrician, general contractor, HVAC contractor, radon service, and landscaper on your referral list. These are all on "my team." Having these reliable people ready to help will provide a welcome stress reliever for your clients, and welcome business for your fellow professionals.

Settlement day!

This is it. The culmination of all the work, all the negotiations, and all the waiting. You're ready to settle. Or are you? I have one absolute rule about settlements: The HUD-1 and the final settlement papers *must* be emailed or faxed to me so that my seller can see them before we go to settlement. I say that my seller will not even leave home to come to settlement until they see that settlement sheet. If the title company doesn't have the settlement sheet, they don't have the complete package and they're not ready. And so there is no point having us sit there waiting for them to get their act together.

Once you have that resolved, you're ready. All the repairs and inspections have been completed, the final walk-through went off without a hitch, and there you are all smiling and gathered around the settlement table. The title company representative and the real estate agents are calm; the buyers and sellers are probably nervous, especially if it's the first time for the buyers. There's coffee, water, and soda for those who want something to drink, and perhaps some jelly beans or M&Ms to keep the energy up. A stack of papers that looks to be about five feet tall awaits you and your clients. One by one, the papers are passed around, read, and signed. Checks change hands. Keys pass from seller to buyer. And then it's over. Handshakes, hugs, sometimes even a little dance for joy signal the time to go.

After the closing, I believe it's very important to break bread with my clients. We'll go out for breakfast, lunch, or dinner, depending on when the settlement is. And if it's not possible directly after closing, then I'll schedule it very soon. I want to give them time to relax after the stress of the closing and to ask me any final questions. Often this turns into a time for them to talk about their dreams and plans that now, finally, can be turned into reality.

I tend not to give a tangible gift to people who are in the middle of moving. Especially if the sellers are older and downsizing, a contribution to their favorite charity might be an alternative. Whether you give a gift or not will depend in part on custom in your area, and in part on your relationship with the clients. Use your own good judgment.

When deals circle the drain

You work for months overcoming all sorts of obstacles and challenges to get a deal through. And finally…it falls apart. When you finish stomping, hissing, or doing whatever you do to let off steam, it's time to remember what is about to be your favorite new four-letter word: N-E-X-T!

I'm not saying this is easy, but it does go better with practice. I had a good example of the need for NEXT not long ago when I had sold a home for a woman who was planning to move out of state. We had a contract for the sale, my seller wrapped up her life in Baltimore, packed up her home, and moved. Everyone was happy. Until the day before settlement, when the buyers announced they decided not to go through with the purchase. They forfeited their $10,000 deposit. Suddenly my seller had to put her home back on the market, this time as an empty house. Not an easy sale, but there we were. NEXT. (Yes, we did sell the house again and it went through fine, but it was tough time for my seller.)

Not every deal is a winner. Not every deal will make it to settlement. Clients fire you, and sometimes you fire a client. (Yes! You do!) Maybe the house won't sell no matter what you try. Perhaps you and your client are the victims of incompetence on someone else's part. Or maybe toxic people on either side just make the whole process so painful that there is no way to reach agreement.

Whatever the reason, there will be times when you need to shut the door and move on. Even if you can still hear and feel the rumbling from behind that closed door, you need to walk away and leave that negative energy- and time-waster behind.

NEXT is a powerful word. Say it aloud and feel that door shut behind you. Now you're facing whatever comes next, not what is over and unrecoverable. When we put our hearts into our work — as we do — it can be very difficult to let go and admit that we can't get a deal done. Intellectually we know that we have to let it go; emotionally it's not that simple. Another way of saying it is: When the horse is dead, dismount! NEXT.

Don't get me wrong. I'm not telling you to walk away when you have been wronged or when your reputation is on the line. You do need to stand up for yourself, especially if someone or some organization such as a rival brokerage is trying to cheat you. For that you fight. You prove you are in the right and you take whatever legal action you need to protect yourself and your business. That's different. NEXT is for those times when it's over and you need to let go of the emotions and hard feelings and move on. NEXT.

The partner of NEXT is something we talked about in Chapter 1 — WIN. And when you think of it, these two work together beautifully. When you ask yourself, **"What's Important Now?"** the honest answer will be to move on to the NEXT opportunity. NEXT has gotten me through a lot in the past 18 plus years. Try it, you'll like it!

And speaking of what's next, in Chapter 7 we'll talk about the one thing we never have enough of.

CHAPTER SIX - LET'S MAKE A DEAL
❑ Choose your clients carefully, and help them prepare for and understand the entire process from contract to settlement.
❑ Build a team of professionals who can provide quick service and quality work at fair prices to your clients.
❑ When deals go bad, move on. Use the power of WIN and NEXT to close doors and open future opportunities for yourself.

SEVEN
MONEY IS ALL YOU NEED...
RIGHT?

If you had all the money you needed, you could do everything you wanted, couldn't you? You could buy the house of your dreams and furnish it the way you want. You could travel around the world or start your own rock band. You could endow a scholarship or become an artist. You could read all the books you've always wanted to or go on an archeological dig. You could spend a month at Canyon Ranch, cruise around the world, or better yet, buy a home on a cruise ship so your home could travel. You could buy or start a real estate brokerage and make it the biggest and best ever. All you need is money.

Did you see the catch in there? Even if you have the money, there's one thing you can't change: time. You get 24 hours each day, just like every other person on this planet. Add time to the picture and now you have to make choices. Do you start a band or a brokerage? Do you teach or travel? What can you do to make the most of the time you have?

As I've said, I decided early in my real estate career to work solo. It had to be my business, and it had to be done my way. But that decision limited my ability to grow and help my clients because I have only those same 24 hours. There's a limit to how much I can get done in a day...or is there?

Solo but not alone

Working solo does not mean working alone. What it does mean is finding ways to build efficiency into what I do. It means finding people with the right skills that I can hand off tasks to and not have to think about them again. It means having assistance, not assistants.

Solo but not alone — that's my answer. But I didn't start out knowing that. For a while I missed or ignored some warning signs that I was going over the edge in my determination to have control of every aspect of my business. (That's one of those less-than-attractive Type E characteristics.)

Details like RSVPs were getting away from me — the business wasn't suffering but some details of my life were crumbling, and I was unintentionally causing stress for other people.

So I started looking at what other agents did. What I found was not answers so much as examples of what I did *not* want to do. I did not want to hire an assistant; that would bring with it obligations as well as legal and financial commitments. That was not how I wanted to run my business. It's all detail stuff, and Type Es are not good at that! At the very least I'd have to hire someone else to keep track of the details about the assistant I didn't want to hire in the first place. Nope, not the answer.

I also did not want to join or start a team. There was no advantage for me in sharing the results of my work with someone else, and I certainly didn't want anyone using my name to expand their business. In a profession where your name is your brand, I knew that having other people representing themselves as being part of my business would be giving away an essential control that I chose not to allow.

The keys to solo success

One of the first things I did was look at how I could build efficiencies into my day. We've already talked about a couple of techniques like getting rid of a pager and not necessarily answering every phone call as it comes in. That does not mean I don't respond, and quickly, but if I'm in the middle of something important, I'll let the call go to voicemail and then call the person back.

This is something I make clear to my clients at the beginning. Almost always my phone will ring during a listing appointment. If it's a phone number I don't recognize, I will take that call. Then I explain to my new client that "it could have been a call on your house," and that I will always take those when working for them. However, if it's a number I recognize, then I don't answer. I explain that people I deal with know how I operate, and that I return all calls and emails. I actually train them that if they leave a message or email, and don't hear back from me, that they should assume I did not get the message.

In this way I educate people to respect my time. The key, of course, is that I *do* return all calls and emails. Buyers, sellers, and other agents learn that they can depend on a response. This puts the control in my hands, not those of the caller. Being available and responsive does *not* mean dropping whatever you are doing to take a phone call that is not a true emergency. It definitely does not mean putting the person I'm talking to on hold so I can take another call. Don't you hate it when you hear that "call waiting" beep on the line, and the person you are talking to says, "hold on a minute" and then disappears? That to me means I'm not important enough to hold their attention, and I don't want other people feeling that way. However, being available *does* mean returning phone calls in a reasonable amount of time, based on the subject and urgency.

When you follow through on communication, your clients don't need to know where you are or what you are doing, so long as the service is there. When I was interviewed for an article and said that I take one week off a month, the magazine's editor called later to check that I really said that. In response, I asked, "Do you know where I am now?" No. And I never did tell her. But she got the point and published the article that way.

While we're talking about phone calls, let's spend a moment on voicemail. We all have that love/hate relationship: we love being able to leave a message, and we hate when we get a message that is long/rambling/garbled/a waste of time. So it's never too late for a refresher on Communication 101. People form an opinion about us by how we communicate. And since time is the one thing we cannot change, it's important to respect the time of the person you are calling.

That person could be the media, could be your seller, or could be a future client. Here are some points to consider before you start recording after the beep. The time saved by these very simple but common sense rules can give you more time for enjoying your real estate business and the rest of your life.

Rants. Sometimes you just have to let off steam, but if you're ever tempted to do it in a voice mail, think "court room." Verbal or written, words live on no matter how much we want to take them back. Rant to your friend or spouse, even write a blistering letter to someone, but don't send it for at least 24 hours. Then wait another 24. Then tear it up and move on. It's very easy to get wound up about a topic and forget that you are speaking to the world. Before you speak, picture what you say as the lead story in your hometown newspaper.

Think it through. Make sure you cover the essentials. A while ago I received a very long phone message with only a first name. I am sure the person thought she left me a number, because the message ended with, "Please call me a soon a possible." I have no clue who that was, and no way to respond. If you get in the habit of saying your name and phone number at the beginning and end of the message, you'll be less likely to forget these essentials.

Bits and pieces. Almost as frustrating as the lack of a phone number is an incomplete one. By now we all know that cell phones can hit dead spots. If you suspect that your message didn't get through, call back and repeat your name and number. Yes, you're in a hurry, but how will it save time if the person can't call you back?

Just the facts, ma'am. When you leave a phone message, keep it clear and simple. Your name, phone number, email if necessary, who you are, and what you want, especially if it's to see a specific property. Believe it or not, many of us have more than one property listed. One of the most frustrating messages to receive is "Call me, I want to show your house." What am I supposed to do with that? The cell phone number is blocked so I can't call back, and I have no idea which property we're talking about. If this person had said which house and when they wanted to show it, then said their phone number, I could have confirmed it with a return call. As it was, that call produced no sale for either of us.

Ramblin'. Get to the point! If I have three phone messages and one of them doesn't have a specific question or reason for the call, which do you think I will return last?

No response required. Some calls don't require a response such as transaction updates. "This is Margaret Rome and I will see you at 3:00 pm at Greenwood for the home inspection." A few seconds and the message is transmitted with complete information.

Who's this? Have you ever had a message on your voice mail where it's clear they didn't listen to your outgoing message first? "This is Dr. So-and-so. It's urgent you call me before your procedure in the morning." Except it didn't get to the right person, the caller didn't leave a number, and who knows what that urgent message was? Before you leave a message, be sure you've got the right number. If you're not sure, dial again and listen.

Say "Thank you." Your mother was right. Say "Thank you" and compliment people who take the time to leave good, complete messages. Who doesn't like to hear appreciation?

Which leads to another issue. I always talk on the phone and leave messages as if somebody else was listening in. You cannot control what's happening on the other end, so assume that your business conversation is not private or that your message will be broadcast because someone hits the "speaker" button. Who could be listening? Perhaps a broker, a journalist looking for a story, a buyer, your seller listening to how you answer the questions about their home, or just a curiosity seeker. Messages last and can come back to haunt you. If you are going to leave a message, do it as if it's going to be played to everyone, because when you leave a message, you lose control of it.

There's one more practice that's been important to my success. I did something you don't often hear about in real estate: I established a waiting list. When I got to the point where I had as many listings as I could handle, I didn't refuse to take people on as clients; I would find out their level of urgency. This works great when someone says, "We're just thinking about selling." Then I can say, "That's wonderful, because I have a waiting list. Let's get you on the list now, and when you're ready to sell, we an get started right away." People who are not in a hurry are glad to work this way because I have built my brand and a reputation that I am worth the wait. On the other hand, if the need is more urgent, I would say, "I'm really busy, but I just had a house that sold, and I can bump you ahead of the other people on my waiting list." That makes them feel pretty special!

Assistants – no. Assistance – yes!

Even after I simplified my day and reduced some stress, there still was an issue; working solo meant there were things that needed to be done, things I did not want to do.

That's when I said an emphatic "No" to assistants, and "Yes" to assistance. What does that mean? I found people who can provide the services I need and work independently. Over time I established relationships with Doug of Electromation.net, a talented Web developer, to maintain my Website. I simply email him my photos and descriptions for a property, and that new listing appears on my Website.

Through the recommendation of a friend, I found Joe of Nenet.net, who hosts my Website, keeps my email working, and helps me with SEO (search engine optimization) — something I don't understand but am glad he does. More than once Joe and Doug have helped me through a computer crisis with their quick and effective response.

You know by now that I believe in the power of advertising to create and reinforce my HomeRome brand. So every week I take a full-page ad in *The Jewish Times*, a local paper that reaches my market. Over time I've developed a great relationship with the advertising department staff, so that now all I have to do is call Karen Bark once a week, tell her what to change, and it's done! I can do it by email, voicemail, or over the phone.

I've had success with other advertising media but have found that some wouldn't work with me my way. They wanted things just so, in their form, and that wasted time that I chose not to use that way. So rather than spend my time trying to fit into their boxes, I pulled my ads. And I've always felt that they lost more by being inflexible than I did by not having those advertising outlets.

Making the best use of assistance is not limited to my business. For instance, I don't open my own mail, and for dinner I make reservations. These and other chores are things that take time I could better use making listing appointments. Those are the things that I'm glad to pay other people to do for me. I do, however, enjoy taking care of our collection of feeders myself, and am rewarded by the watching the birds flock to them.

How can you tell if you need assistance in your business? Obviously, if you are constantly stressed due to time pressure, or because the realities of your life mean that you can't get everything done in 24 hours and still have time to eat and sleep, then you need to give yourself a break.

This is when you go back to what we talked about in Chapter 1, and ask yourself that essential question: **What's Important Now?** Once you decide that it's time to get assistance, there's a new set of questions:

- Of all the things that are pressing on you, which *must* you do yourself, legally and ethically?
- Which tasks are repetitive — what do you do more or less the same way every week or month or every time you take a listing or go to settlement?
- What are the things that need to be done but that you really don't like handling?
- What do you put off as long as possible, and sometimes for too long?

When you are used to doing it all yourself, your first reaction might be, "I have to do it all! There's nothing anyone else can do as well as I do!" That might be true, but I'll guarantee you there are things someone else can do that will be different but not different enough to make a difference in your overall success. I could take my time making new pages for my Website each time I take a listing, and I might like them better. But will anyone but me know the difference? Will it sell the home faster to have a fancier Web page, or should I spend my time actually talking to people about the house? WIN?

Or suppose I spent one morning a week tweaking my print ads until they were just exactly perfect to my eye. Would that generate any business? Would that bring more buyers to my listings? Would my business benefit from that activity as much as, say, taking another listing or two? WIN?

Finding the right assistance

Now that you've decided you need to hand off some tasks, and accepted that your business will do better when you do so, how do you decide who will do what? Where do you find people you can trust to give you their best? Think back just one chapter to where we talked about the people you recommend for carpet, roofing, etc. You built a list over time based on your experiences and the recommendations of others. Your colleagues also have Web developers, writers, virtual assistants, cleaning services, and such in their networks — so ask. Look within your social and business networking groups like Active Rain to find individuals and services that offer what you need.

Afraid of choosing the wrong one? Start small and see how it goes. You don't move in with someone after one date; you don't turn over your Website maintenance to a developer until you've tested the service, ability, and responsiveness. Sure, it will take some of your precious time at first, but like everything else in real estate, you're investing in creating a long term relationship. If it doesn't work out, there's always that new favorite four-letter word: NEXT. Move on and find another.

After you've pried the first couple of tasks away from yourself and handed them off to others, you'll find it becomes easier with each step. And sometimes it's a simple matter of necessity or of the need being imposed from outside. It worked that way for me with this book. I realized I could publish it myself if I wanted to. I could get someone to design the cover, someone else to edit and set up the pages, to print it, arrange for shipments, marketing, and all the other chores. But I'm a Type E! I'm the one with the ideas. I needed someone else to make all the details happen. So I helped my friend — who is also a Type E, but a translator — create The Silloway Press, with my book as its first title release.

When you are looking around for assistance, don't overlook your clients. I had a client who bought the purple home that everyone said was unsalable; Lauren Montillo became a friend and is now a business partner. Through Lauren I met Tom Gimer who would become my real estate broker. It started as a lunch meeting to see if Lauren should hang her new license with him, but by the end of the meal we were talking about a new business model that became TRAC, a Realtor®-friendly auction company. To find assistance, you don't need to run ads or look in Craig's list; you can find assistance if you are aware of what's going on around you.

By keeping an open mind and a creative approach, you can maximize your time without reducing your level of service a bit. All it takes is recognizing an opportunity when it calls.

It was pouring down rain when I got the call on one of my properties. It hadn't rained in Baltimore for months, but now when we finally had a good, hard, rain…someone was driving around looking at houses and had seen my sign!

The one he called about had just gone to settlement, and he was disappointed when I told him that it was no longer on the market. Of course, it was then the perfect house, the perfect location, the perfect price — everything he wanted. And, he was qualified for exactly what that house was going for.

An interested buyer is not someone you let wander off. But he was out there in the rain, and I was home and dry. So I asked, did he have time to view a few other properties? Yep, he had time. So I gave him directions, turn right, and go to this property. Turn left on Greenwood and right on Upland to another. Back to Milford and take a right to a third house. I stayed on the phone and "drove" him to all three of my other listings within the same zip code.

As he approached each property, I was able to answer all his questions such as age, condition, number of bedrooms, type of heat, room sizes, additions, upgrades, price, etc. This remote control touring seemed to be better than sending him back home to look at the Website. After all, he was in his car even though it was raining, and thankfully I could give directions.

He seemed to really like the third property. He asked for the size of the yard, so I stayed on the phone with him while he walked around the house, and I described everything to him from the parking pad to the storage shed, and he could see the large level backyard. No, I don't usually suggest that buyers walk on properties, but with my permission and with me on the phone, no problem. He was extremely appreciative. I asked if he was working with an agent, and when the answer was affirmative, I suggested that the agent call me to set up an appointment.

Even if his agent never called, look how much time was saved. By being flexible and adjusting to his needs and the opportunity, we both came out ahead. I'm not sure what to call this kind of showing. It's not a virtual tour. Maybe a remote tour? Driving tour? Flexitour? Whatever name we give it, I think of it as a Type E showing — effective, efficient, and a time saver. Plus, I didn't have to go out in a downpour!

Whether you choose to be a solo-but-not-alone agent, elect to be part of a team, or decide you want to have employees who work only for you, it's all a matter of choosing the way of working that is best for you. Take the time to step back and ask yourself the questions, and then listen to the answers. What are the things that you do best? What are the things that you really like to do and don't want to give up? Where do you feel you waste time or just don't get enough return for the time you invest?

When you have those answers, make your plan and take action. Try what you think will work best for a few months, then step back and ask, "How am I doing?" If you are working with less stress and more accomplishment, keep it up. If not, go back and ask yourself the questions again, make adjustments, and keep at it until you find the balance that's right for you and your business. Above all, do only what you want and like to do.

Next up: the one subject that can make even seasoned professionals wonder if they know enough.

CHAPTER SEVEN – MONEY IS ALL YOU NEED ... RIGHT?
❏ No matter how long you've been a real estate professional, you can improve your effectiveness and efficiency by managing time better.
❏ Consider what tasks you *must* do and which you can delegate, then hire the right assistants or find the right assistance to make better use of your time.
❏ If you choose to work as a solo agent, find assistance to complement and augment your strengths. You'll reduce your stress level and increase your production while enjoying it more.

EIGHT
MARKETING MATTERS

Say "marketing" and some people shudder as if it's a curse or a demon. Mature, successful business people will tell you, "I can talk to 200 people, but I don't really feel I understand the best way to market." The truth is, they would never get the chance to talk to those 200 people, or even one prospect, unless they were successful at marketing.

A quick search of the Internet will prove that there are thousands of "experts" ready to sell you the latest marketing technique, but how do you choose what's best for you and your business?

Let's begin by saying what real estate marketing is and is not. Marketing your real estate business *is:*

- creating an awareness of you and Brand YOU (remember Chapter 3?),
- letting people know what you do,
- educating people on the advantages and value of using your services,
- supporting your image as an honest, ethical, contributing member of your community,

- something you do every day,
- focused on the needs of your clients and prospects.

Marketing your real estate business is *not*:
- just advertising (advertising is part of it, but not all of it),
- high pressure sales,
- handing your business card to every person you meet whether they want it or not,
- something you do once in a while,
- focused on what you might get out of every prospect.

Anne Hruby, my friend and first real estate trainer, told me, "There are no hard and fast rules about successful marketing in real estate. It's not so much the 'what' you choose to do as the 'how' you do it, and the fact that you follow through."

You really cannot tell if a person is a buyer or a seller just by looking at them; you have to let everyone know what you do. The challenge is to market yourself and your brand in a consistent way that reflects your personality and style and that will create the impression you want. It is my job is to let them know I'm in real estate; it's not their job to remember me.

It's no secret that salespeople can come on strong and don't always seem to have their buyers' and sellers' best interests at heart. No one wants to feel as if their only value is the money they can put in your pocket. No one wants to be seen as one more potential commission. But you can quickly overcome any negative preconceptions that people have by demonstrating that you are not that stereotype. How? By following the basic premise of Floyd Wickman's philosophy: You get by giving.

Give information
Not long ago, Realtors® were the gatekeepers for all information

on real estate. They knew what houses were for sale and where. They knew what houses sold for and how long they were on the market. They alone had access to the multiple list service.

No more. Today, the majority of homebuyers research houses online before ever talking with a real estate agent. If you want to reach those potential clients, you need to be where they are, and you need to make it easy for them to find out about you and your listings, or any listings.

If you go to a Website and you don't see what you are looking for, what do you do? You go somewhere else.

If you think you find what you are looking for, but the site insists on you giving personal information before you can go any further, what do you do? Many people will refuse and go find a site where they don't have to leave contact information. These potential clients are not stupid; they know that leaving a phone number means you will probably try to call them. They don't want to give up that control.

That's why I make it easy for anyone who visits my Website to see not only my listings but also any listing in the multiple list without giving any information at all. I found that buyers and sellers, as well as agents when they are not in the office, will use my site to search the multiple list. As they navigate through the site, they will see my name, my email address, my phone number, and my face. They will be reminded who is making their search easy and anonymous.

Buyers can see what's available in the areas they are interested in. But savvy sellers also use this to see what's going on in their neighborhood. Then I make it easy for a visitor to get in touch with me by email or phone. And I certainly don't mind making things easier for an agent if everything comes with my name and number on it.

Give assistance

The phone rings. I answer, "Hi, this Margaret."

"How much is the house on Taney Road?"

"$259,944" I answer.

"How many bedrooms?"

"Four"

"Is the basement finished?"

"There is no lower level."

"Why is it priced like that?"

"It is being sold 'As Is'"

"How much work does it need?"

"Windows, new kitchen, bathrooms, it needs total renovation."

Yes, I answer questions about my listings. I answer without asking the caller's name, qualifications, or motives. I give information whenever asked.

You may ask, "Why do you do that?" After all, agents are trained to get information, like how much someone makes, and where do they work. Maybe not on the first call, but agents need this information so they can follow up. That means calling at dinnertime to find out if the prospect is still looking for a house.

Years ago, when I was looking for a home, I would see a "For Sale" sign and call to ask price, number of bedrooms, does it have a fireplace, etc. I did *not* get answers — I got questions: "Where do you live? How much do you want to spend for a house? ...." And the follow up phone calls were intolerable. Back in the days before caller ID, I learned to change my name and phone number when I was asked.

Later, when I got into real estate, I vowed that I would not treat the public this way. I give out addresses, I give out price, I answer all their questions. In fact, I tell the caller up front that I will not ask for their name, and they can ask me anything. I tell them it is OK if they are working with another agent, I will still give them all the answers about my listings.

I tell them about my Website http://www.homerome.com where they can go to see my listings — all of them have interior photos. I don't ask for anything but email address, and then only if they want daily notifications. I make it simple with these directions:

"You can find every active listing in the multiple listing service (MLS) by going to www.HomeRome.com and clicking on ALL LISTINGS. Be sure to put in your email, search criteria such as type of home and price range. You will receive daily updates of properties that meet your needs, including photos, address, price, etc. This free service will make finding your special home easier."

Buyers use this site, sellers use this site, and friends, family, and even other agents use this site. Anyone can keep up with all the active listings without having to talk with an agent.

Why would I do this? Because I have had wonderful success and love this real estate business. I don't "go after" the business; it comes to me by doing things this way. Many times the callers are so impressed with my willingness to share that they want me to take their information. They want to work with me. It seems the harder I try not to get invasive with questions, the more they choose to share with me.

It happened again when a woman found one of my new listings on the Internet. The caller from Texas only asked a couple of questions and didn't give her name. As I answered, we both realized this was not the home she needed for her family. Yes, it was in the right location and it was in the right price range, but it was certainly not large enough for her family of four children.

Before our conversation was finished, she wanted to know if I would consider helping her find a home when her family moved to Baltimore. She said she never had an agent be so forthright with information, and she wanted to work with me. This is the kind of buyer I want to work with.

When I started in real estate, I made that promise to give information freely because I didn't like how I was treated. Now I tell any caller anything they want to know about a property, and send them to my Website for details and photos. After many years and hundreds of transactions, I'm convinced it's still the best way to build trust and confidence -and the business keeps coming.

Make it easy for people to do business with you by being available. Remember I said in Chapter 2 that I make my own appointments? Over the years I've found that being available this way saves time and aggravation for everyone. As the listing agent, I'm the person who knows the property best and can ask a potential buyer questions like, "What is the most important thing you're looking for in a house?" Of course the listing has all the features of the property, but only the personal conversation can find out what matters to each buyer. And this can only happen if the agent is available to answer questions and book appointments.

Use technology

A computer cannot list or sell a house, but it can streamline the process in many ways. It's important to have a welcoming Website that is easy to navigate and to keep it up-to-date. When you give people useful tools that make the process easy for them, they come back again and again. (Read more about using technology in Chapter 9.) Here are some examples:

- **Buyers4YourHome.com.** I originated this idea and created a page on my Website that allows people to tell the world what they are looking for in a home. People email me what they want, I put it on the site, and potential sellers can scan for a match. I prefer to work with sellers, but buyers also have homes to sell and I don't want to turn them away empty handed.

■ **My listings.** Every one of my listings has a separate page on the Website that buyers can download, print, and carry with them as they drive around. The page includes the basic information on the house plus plenty of photos and a narrative description that brings emotion into the process by describing not only the rooms but also how the potential homeowner might enjoy them.

■ **My blogs.** Yes, that's blogs, plural. ~~One Weblog is on Active Rain, the other is on the Blogger platform.~~ On both I talk about what's happening in the Baltimore market, discuss local events or area day trips, and let people know about what's happening in my (public) life. Some articles (posts) are just informative, but I also have conversation starters. One time I used a contest to raise interest in a unique property that I had listed, that historic church that had been converted into a residence and artist's studio (Chapter 5). The contest asked readers to come up with ideas for creative uses for the building, with the winner being announced in my blog and on the Sunday afternoon radio show that I often host. The response was great, and we got more people talking about this "difficult" property.

■ **Join the ActiveRain Real Estate Network,** an online community of real estate professionals. You'll find a dynamic group with members around the country who are eager to share advice and experiences to help everyone improve. Your blog on Active Rain can bring you recognition with buyers and sellers as well as other real estate agents around the country. I've received referrals from agents in other parts of the country just because of Active Rain. You'll find more about Active Rain in Chapter 7. ~~Use this link to get started: http://activerain.com/action/blogs_admin/referrals/homerome.~~

You never know when a casual conversation that starts by talking about technology will turn into a wonderful connection. My first blog started in San Antonio while I was at the Cyber-Star® Summit. For three days I immersed myself in high energy multi-tasking, surrounded by the best of the best in the real estate business.

On the flight back to Baltimore I was working on my tablet PC as usual, reading through my notes, and I started chatting with the woman in the next seat. (The tablet is a great conversation-starter — better than a dog, and you don't have to clean up after it!) She said she was going to visit her sister-in-law who has a cleaning business in Maryland. I asked her name, and in a city of several hundred thousand, of course I know her sister-in-law. We met several years ago through NAWBO, (National Association of Women Business Owners). With the tablet's note-taking feature, I was able to have my seatmate write her name and email address right on the tablet's screen.

Six months later I heard from her again. She'd been thinking about looking for another house, and she said she would move if she could find a good agent. Did I know anyone? Of course! I was delighted to put her in touch with the CyberStar® in San Antonio, Christina Whipple.

You just never know when the person next to you will turn into a new client for you or a connection for someone else. It's all about being open to the possibility — and the fun — of a conversation with someone new.

Give time and effort

Do you look for opportunities to help people out? Do you join and participate actively in groups in your industry, such as Active Rain, CyberStars®, CyberPros™, Women's Council of REALTORS®, ACRE™? And how about business groups such as networking groups like NAWBO? All of these take some investment of time and effort, but that's how relationships are built. It's only when you get involved — doing more than attending an occasional meeting — that you get the real benefit of being part of a group of like-minded professionals.

Sometimes people who are new to real estate worry about net-working. You know it's important because you have to let people know what you do. But you can't just walk up to someone and say, "Hi, do you want to buy or sell a house?" You also can't wander through a networking event handing your card to everyone there. Well, you can, but it's not a good idea. What you can do is talk to people.

Get out of your office. Get face-to-face. Do you have kids? Go to their games and activities. Remember everyone needs to live somewhere. Join and take part in the activities that you enjoy. It's easy to start a conversation.

If you're new to networking, just remember to ask about the other person first. What do they do? How did they get into that business? What kind of client are they looking for? One of the best ways to receive referrals is to first provide referrals. Who do you know who might be a good connection for the person you have just met? Offer to introduce them if you genuinely believe you have at least a potential match for either new business or a cooperative working situation. Ask, "How can I help you?"

When you show genuine interest in someone they will almost certainly ask about your business and give you a chance to present your elevator speech (Chapter 3). That's when you can expand on your business and talk about a recent success; everyone likes success stories. I don't believe in giving my business card to everyone I talk to. That is not how you build your brand as a resource for valuable real estate information. If someone hands me their card when I didn't ask for it, that card is probably going in the trash. On the other hand, if I see that I might be able to help someone with a potential client or a resource for their business, I enter their information into my Treo and follow up later.

One way I invest is by taking the time on many Sundays to host a radio show, *All About Real Estate* on Baltimore's 680 WCBM. This gives me an opportunity to talk about my listings, the market, or anything that listeners call in about. Usually I have at least one guest, and it's always fun. If you're not the microphone type, why not write articles for your local newspaper or offer to present a seminar at your local board of Realtors®? They all serve to increase visibility for Brand YOU.

Give appreciation

Remember that a small gesture goes a long way. How many thank-you notes have you written this week? Do you have nice-looking thank-you notes? Do you have them with you, with stamps, so it is easy to take a few minutes to show your appreciation for someone who has made your day a bit better? Sure, I send thanks by email, but a physical card in an envelope is likely to be remembered.

I recently found a solution that suits my Type E personality for sending cards. I signed up with SendOutCards and now have access to literally thousands of cards covering every type of situation from new baby to new home. With a SendOutCards account, you choose your card online, write your own message, add your own signature, and send it out in minutes. You save time and still have the same effect as a card in an envelope with a stamp.

Something else you can do is to start (or join) a mentor group. If you don't have a group, begin with an agent you admire and respect and ask what you can do to help them in their business. If there's a new agent who wants to learn from you, invite them to "shadow" you for a day or two. Offer to cover for them for a couple of hours whenever they need you. You'll both learn something, and you might be helping a future real estate success take their first steps on the road.

Add creative marketing

It doesn't matter what kind of market it is; creativity raises your visibility. You don't need to be a marketing genius or have an un-limited budget. In fact, looking for small things you can do that make you memorable is one of the most effective ways of build-ing awareness of Brand YOU. All it takes is an open mind and a willingness to see things differently. Like, for instance, my "Mono-grammed Candy."

> *At a CyberStars® conference focused on advertising, my pre-sentation was "Finding Your Sweet Spot in Advertising: The Best of Free and Best of Paid." Not long before that I had written a blog post about a candy shop in Atlantic City, NJ, named "It's Sugar." That's where I found my signature candy — brown (my favorite color) M&Ms, each with an "M" on it. One of my points was that you need to find something unique to promote yourself. It doesn't have to be expensive and you can have fun with it. So the night before the pre-sentation I took a bunch of small plastic bags filled with the brown M&Ms and tied each with a brown ribbon. As I was*

> talking about my very own monogrammed candy, I started tossing the individual bags out to the CyberStars. My aim was not too good, but they got the point.

You can also take something ordinary, reframe it with your signature, and create a unique marketing piece. I discovered the Roomba robotic vacuum cleaner and adopted it as my new housekeeper. He's wider than he is tall, but he works like a charm. Never complains, just gets down to work vacuuming every floor in the house making sure to get close to the walls as he goes. Needs absolutely no supervision either; he just does his thing and then goes home and parks and recharges. When the Roomba is working, I feel like I'm in a Jetsons episode!

After watching the robot vacuum do his job for a while, I realized he would make a terrific settlement gift for my sellers. I don't always give gifts, but if I gave a Roomba I would add a label to change his name to ROMEba, and they would never forget my name.

Look for something unique in your community or area of the country. Even if the idea doesn't work for you, it could spark another idea. Here in Maryland, I'm thinking a crab feast or bull roast might be attractive; wouldn't it be nice to walk out of a settlement knowing that your housewarming party is already catered? Water-loving clients might be tempted by a sunset cruise and overnight stay — a "Boat & Breakfast" — on a schooner out of historic Annapolis. Whether it's a local food specialty or hard-to-get tickets, your state probably has something unique that would make a great, attention-grabbing incentive.

Jay Burnham in Massachusetts has capitalized on a couple of current hot topics — the cost of gas and protecting the environment — by offering a Segway Personal Transporter at closing to qualifying home sellers who list with him.

make a meal + Drop it off - come back later for dishes

With his "Great Segway Giveaway" program, not only did Jay help sellers reduce their carbon footprint, he also received positive press coverage for both his business and his commitment to a green lifestyle. "The Segway Personal Transporter is a clean, green, eco-friendly machine that gets the energy equivalency of 450 miles to the gallon and therefore saves me hundreds of dollars a year in fuel costs by using it to commute to work and to shopping," said Burnham. "I launched this program to personally tout the benefits of using a Segway, and to also help my customers obtain the same benefits that I have received since owning one. They are also easy and fun to ride."

You are unique. There are hundreds of thousands of other real estate agents in the country and world, but there is only one you. To have a successful marketing program, find ways to attach characteristics that are yours alone to your brand.

One of the things I did early on was link my listings to a specific number. If you notice, almost *all* listing prices end in 000, 500, or 900. I chose to make my listings more visible by using the same number unique to me in each one.

Back then I was driving my little dream car, a Porsche 944, and I began using this number on my first listing. Now I use it on all my listings. When you look down a column of listings or sales and see some that end with 944 … yep, those are mine.

I find that the number gets noticed by lenders and title attorneys as well as other agents. If you go to www.Realtor.com and put in my zip code, 21209, pictures of four "Featured Homes" will come up; one will always be mine. How can you tell which one? It's the one that ends with "944."

I once went on a listing appointment but chose not to work with that seller — he wanted full service for a no-service commission. A short time later, I got a call from an agent asking if I was a partner of agent "X." When I asked why, I was told he was

last 3 digits of my phone # 944

using "my" number. He took my "rejected" listing but used my suggested price ending in 944. When I spoke to that agent, he told me that I could *not* own a number. I just thanked him because I was getting calls from other agents about this property, but they only wanted to work with me! He changed the sales price in the MLS that same day. And 944 is still "my" number.

Next time you take a listing, try making the price a unique number — one that means something to you — and see what happens.

Color outside the lines

It's another version of that cliché, thinking outside the box. Do you assume that every house that's for sale is also in the multiple list? Of course not. If that's true, then there must be houses that are *not* for sale now, but *could* be for sale if the right buyer appeared. Here's one approach I've used, and yes, it does work!

> *In a buyer's market, there is way too much inventory and too many houses that are not selling. But still, I had good, qualified buyers who needed a special home.*
>
> *One such family was a blended family. Mother, father, total of four children. Each parent was married before and each had two kids. So we didn't just need a new house, we needed the perfect home. Each child was promised their own room. After all, they each had their own rooms prior to the remarriage; why should they be penalized because of the family blending? And with such a large family, and both parents working, an au pair was essential.*
>
> *So now we were up to six bedrooms. We needed to find the right home in the right school system, and you guessed it, those needs don't always match up. There was another challenge, too. With a price range of $500,000 to $750,000, you'd say we had a generous budget, but we also had a lot of*

specs to satisfy. We needed a kid-friendly neighborhoo
sidewalks and places to ride bikes. We needed a neig.
hood with charm and character, and houses with style —
clone-onials, no tract houses. The kitchen had to be big and
warm and friendly, and be a place for meals, homework,
and gatherings — in other words the hub of the house. There
needed to be room to "get away" with kids' space and adult
space. That's not all! It had to be in the northern part of Baltimore County or in northwest Baltimore City. Easy access
to the Baltimore Beltway was a must.

I placed an "ad" on my www.buyers4yourhome.com and
made up flyers for the buyers to leave at homes they were
interested in. The flyer read:

"Dear Home Owner, Our family would like to live in this
neighborhood. We like your home and if you are thinking of
selling, please contact our real estate agent: Margaret Rome,
TREC — The Real Estate Company of Maryland, 410-530-
2400 or mrome@homerome.com Fax: 866-806-2353. All
calls are confidential."

I gave the buyers a batch of flyers to keep in their cars.
When they saw a home they both liked, they could slip the
flyer inside the screen door. I instructed them to let me know
which homes they were interested in so I could be prepared
when the call came in. I could do the research in advance
— how much it was assessed for, how long the present owner
had lived there, taxes, comps etc.

Why wait for the perfect home to come on the market?
Anyone can wait for a home to show up in the MLS. Be pro-
active! Some sellers may be holding back, thinking they will
wait until the market gets better. Just because it's not in the
MLS, don't assume a home isn't for sale, especially if it seems
like the perfect home for your buyers.

In another example of both creative thinking and the strength of relationships in this business, Ira Serkes, my good friend and fellow CyberStar® in Berkeley, CA, made a connection with *Wall Street Journal* reporter, Bob Hagerty. Hagerty heard Ira's presentation at an Inman Real Estate Convention and later called Ira as a source for his article on creative ways to find homes for buyers during a seller's market. Ira gave Hagerty my name as another source. And this was the result in the Journal's online article, "Make Me an Offer: Buying Unlisted Homes":

> "Margaret Rome…in Baltimore, once ran an ad in the Baltimore Jewish Times announcing that one of her buyers was seeking a "funky" four-bedroom ranch house in a particular school district for less than $400,000. An owner of such a house, which wasn't yet listed, responded, and a sale was quickly arranged, Ms. Rome says."

So you see, marketing really is everything you do in your business. It's as much a state of mind as it is the specific things you do to be known as the best real estate agent in the area. It takes time and effort, but the payoff is in taking your success to a new level. Whether the real estate market is up or down, you must continue to market yourself and advertise. You can look for low cost alternatives such as volunteering to host a radio show or increasing your presence on real estate networking Websites like Active Rain. But mostly you can be consistent in thinking of what you can do to help your clients.

Remember the book *Who Moved My Cheese?* Well, Floyd Wickman once said to me, "I don't care *who* moved it. I just want to go find it." Go find your "cheese!" Go out and get your business, your buyers, and your sellers.

Now, before we get into one of my favorite topics in Chapter 9, let's recap:

CHAPTER EIGHT – MARKETING MATTERS
☐ Marketing is what you do every day to build and reinforce your brand as a successful professional.
☐ Marketing does not have to be expensive; low cost, creative ideas can be very successful.
☐ Whatever marketing techniques you use, consistency is essential. Every day ask yourself, "What can I do for someone today?" Then do it.

NINE
TECH SAVVY OR GADGET ADDICT?

When you start out in real estate these days you are told that you need many things. At the top of the list are all the technology re-lated "must have"s like a multi-function phone, email, a Website, a digital camera, and any number of other gadgets. But there is a difference between "must have" and "good for your business." You don't always need that latest gadget.

What Realtors® do is actually very low tech. We list, sell, and get to the settlement table. That's it. When speaking to new agents I hold up a blank sheet of paper and a pen, and say, "These are all I really need to do my job." You don't need technology to network and meet people. You don't need technology to listen to sellers talk about their home. A computer can show you photos but it cannot show a house with the warmth and personality needed to have that buyer already living in the property. All that creativity, and the personal approach, must come from the agent first. Please don't ever lose sight of this.

Having said that, it's also true that using technology — the right technology — makes my life simpler and my work more ef-fective. It saves me time and allows me to have more personal time. And it does all this without me being tied to an office. Had I not found the right tech tools for my business, I would not have been able to work solo. That's the *real* advantage of technology today.

Top tech tools

As you get into real estate, you will hear many opinions about the best technology tools and services. Everyone you talk to seems to have a favorite "I couldn't do business without it" tool. Before you invest in anything, take your time to read and learn about the plusses and minuses. Even a gadget that works perfectly may not be right for you if it doesn't save you time or make you more efficient. Maybe it's just the newest or most fun; that's fine, too, but make sure you're well informed before you hand over your credit card!

I have my Top Ten, of course — those things I couldn't and wouldn't want to do business without.

1. Multi-function phone. Mine is a Treo™, other people have BlackBerrys®, iPhones, or other brands. The most important questions to ask are:

- Will it automatically sync to my computer, creating a constantly updated backup?
- Does it have all the features I want and need?
- Would I be paying for features that I would not need or use?
- Is the screen large enough to read easily?
- Is the keypad (actual or on screen) easy to use?
- Does the phone have Bluetooth˙ so I can use it while driving?
- If and when I want a new phone, can I easily move all my information from the old one to a new one?

Whether you call it a cell phone or a PDA (personal digital assistant), you'll find this tech tool essential in today's real estate business. The important thing is to find one that works for you.

Some people love the iPhone but I wouldn't use all its options, so I stick with my Treo™. I like using my fingernail on the screen and keys; other people don't like the Treo™ because the buttons are small. You need to find the phone that is most comfortable for you and that you will use. For some, having a PDA and a separate phone may be the best.

I used to take my computer with me everywhere, but since my phone now has email, instant messaging, and internet access, my phone is my computer when I'm on the go.

2. Laptop computer. Several years ago I discovered the tablet computer, and have used one ever since. The handwriting and recording alone is worth the price. With this I can have listing agreements and contracts signed on the spot and emailed immediately to everyone involved. I used to say, "Have Tablet Will Travel." In the first few months I had this wonderful machine, it became a part of me. My work life changed dramatically, and it made things better for me and my clients.

One of my favorite features is handwriting. That's right, good old-fashioned pen to paper writing. Except now, it's stylus to screen. The first time I tried writing on my tablet's screen I was laughing like a kid with her first Magic Slate. My handwriting, right there, on the screen! And I can make it bolder, change color, and even erase.

So what happens next? Can a computer really read and save my writing? Yes, it can read and convert my writing to printed text. But what's even better is this:

Have tablet will travel!

That was written on my tablet and sent by email to end up in this book. Can't you just see the possibilities? Signed listings and offers on the spot. A personal note of thanks to an appraiser or inspector. A quick message to a friend. I use this feature often and still get a kick out of it. And on days when I'm on the road a lot, I think this tablet is one of the best investments I've ever made next to my Treo.

Whether you choose a tablet or a more conventional laptop, some of the features you'll want are:

- Wifi capability built in — most come with this, but check to be sure.
- An add-on air card — a plug in card or device that lets you connect to the Internet wherever you are. It's like having a little cell phone dedicated to your computer. Yes, it has a monthly fee, but for a real estate agent on the move, you need to be connected whenever and wherever you are.
- Anti-virus software that will automatically scan incoming emails and files and that will not interfere with other software you may be running.
- A lightweight but protective carrying case. With the tablet, I have what they call a "bump case" that protects the computer edges, and I added a flap of leather to protect the screen along with a leather pouch that holds the essentials like the mini-mouse, power cord, and air card.
- If you are going to use the computer outside, a "view anywhere" screen is important so that you can read the display easily in sunlight.

My tablet PC has been essential to solo success. Here's a good example:

> *By eight on a Monday morning I was on a train for a quick day trip to New York City. By evening I was back. And though I talked to several people, made appointments, did some negotiating, and read and sent emails, most people never knew I'd left.*
>
> *Dawn was just breaking when we got to Penn Station in Baltimore, and I couldn't resist snapping some photos of the classic façade. It reminds me of a grand hotel from the turn of the 20th century.*
>
> *With camera stowed we boarded the train and I settled in. My tablet PC plugged into the seat outlet, and with my cell phone handy, I made all my appointments and then scheduled one settlement for Thursday and another one for Friday afternoon. After that, it was negotiation for a home inspection, and then I downloaded the photos I took of the station.*
>
> *When we rolled into New York's Penn Station we found a charming porter to help us. They really do make it easy to get to and from the Big Apple by train.*
>
> *Our day's errands done, we came back home with the same ease. All the way I was keeping up with phone calls and emails. With the right technology it didn't matter where I was — it was business as usual.*
>
> *Sing it with me... "I've been workin' on the railroad!"*

3. Website. You already know that every real estate agent needs a good Website. You cannot seriously call yourself a professional these days without one. If you need to, go back and re-read the section in Chapter 3 on Websites. What makes a good Website? There are many people who are experts, but here's what I think are the essentials:

- It should be easy to understand and navigate. When people visit your site they need to understand immediately that they are in the right place.

- Give information without insisting on getting any personal information up front. People are more and more careful about giving even an email address as spam and phishing fill their inboxes. There are plenty of places people can go to get listing information, so don't push them away. Make it easy to find what they are looking for, and they'll stay around.

- Make it attractive, clean, and easy to read. Have you ever landed on a Website where you couldn't figure out what to look at first because there was so much on the page? If you're anything like me, you'll give it a few seconds and go somewhere else. The lesson here: don't try to put everything in front of your visitor at once. Instead, lead them with clear links or icons.

- Add features that help your visitors. Think about what people might want when they come to your site, and give it to them quickly. With so much information available on houses for sale, it's easy to be completely wrapped up in finding that perfect home for your family. But what about finding someone to buy your home?

> *My Buyers4YourHome.com page is a good example. You recall that I set up this page on my Website to help sellers see if there is someone already looking for a house like theirs.*
>
> *Buyers send me a wish list — what they are looking for in a home, what area, what price—and I post it on my site. It might be land in Baltimore County or a condo in the city; it could be a ranch house in Green Spring Valley or a townhouse in Pikesville. Sometimes it's as unique as "a*

funky house" or a renovated barn. It includes information about area, price range, school system, and other features the buyer is seeking. Whatever people want, that's what goes on the list. Of course the description is anonymous to protect buyers' privacy, and there's no cost and no obligation.

Homeowners who are thinking of selling can go right to the Buyers4YourHome.com page and see if there is someone looking for their home's style, price, or location. Before they even sign the listing agreement, they call me, and if we find a match, a home may be listed and sold in the same day! Even other agents use it.

When I first created the page, some people thought it was a slightly crazy idea. Now, after several years, the Buyers4YourHome page is one of the most visited on my site.

Another feature of my site that is very popular with sellers is that the individual listing pages are formatted so that they are full-color flyers. Sellers never run out of flyers if they have a color printer; they can download and print off their home's details and photos any time. The same thing works for other agents, and potential buyers can print all the information and carry it with them when they visit.

4. Digital camera. Today's cameras are small and powerful. Something that fits comfortably in a pocket will take high-resolution photos for use in your listings.

- You don't need the latest and greatest, though it can be hard to resist for a techno-addict. (I call mine a "PhD" camera—"Push here, Dummy!")
- Be sure the camera you choose has a simple-to-use download feature to get photos from the camera to your computer quickly.

- Before you leave the store, be sure you know how to use all the features that matter to you. (Later you can learn the others if you have time and interest, but you probably won't get around to it.)
- Take your camera with you everywhere. You never know when you will see something that will make a great photo and that can become a blog article.

5. Weblog (Blog). Right up there in importance with your Website is your blog (or blogs). People may go to your Website to find properties and read about your experience, but in your blog, they will be able to learn about you as well as your listings. So when you blog, there are two things you must do: be yourself, and be consistent.

- By writing naturally about your business, your community, and as much as you want to about your life, you are showing yourself as a real person. You help people become comfortable with you even before they meet you, and that makes things go more smoothly when you finally meet.
- Blogging is something you need to commit a certain amount of time to every week; many people do it every day, and some do it several times a day. Whatever works best for you is fine, but you must post articles to your blog regularly.
- Where you blog is also important. There are probably thousands of sites that you could join as a real estate agent, and there are literally billions of individual blogs. As I said, I'm a big fan of Active Rain, a social network and marketing platform for real estate professionals that was launched in June 2006. In less than two

years they gained over 100,000 members, and it is still growing as this is written. Active Rain helps agents to create business relationships both within the industry and with the consumer. When you join Active Rain, you "meet" real estate professionals from all over the country. Many have very active blogs, and are happy to share experiences, insights, and advice. Within Active Rain are thousands of "groups" where people with like interests gather electronically. I strongly recommend you join Active Rain to raise your visibility in both the profession and with potential clients. Use this link: http://activerain.com/action/referrals/homerome, and I'll be welcoming you to play in the Rain.

- Active Rain has some "Members Only" features for people in the real estate industry, but most blogs on Active Rain can be read by anyone, including buyers and sellers. So yes, put your listings there as well. Then you can write blogs about your listings that present the property and your sellers in an interesting way. Your sellers will love it, and potential buyers have another opportunity to see the property. The key is to focus on something interesting about the house or its contents. For example, the things that homeowners collect can make a house more attractive, or at the very least memorable. This is how I highlighted one of my favorites:

> *The first time I showed the property it was to a fellow agent. What I didn't know was that my sellers had a love for frogs. They had collectible frogs scattered everywhere throughout the 10,000 square foot contemporary home! It reminded me of other collections I've seen in homes over the years, everything from turtles to trains, and hippos to giraffes, and now frogs.*

> *I had to smile each time I saw another example, and each frog in the home had a story. One even lit up at night, and I noticed a great big Christmas frog stored in the carriage house. The owner's favorite was a fat happy fellow who sat in the marble foyer as a greeter, but I have to say mine was the guy in the hammock outside, kicking back and enjoying life.*

As you see, it's a low-key way of highlighting features of the home and keeping it all un-salesy.

6. GPS. Even if you are not directionally challenged, having a GPS in your car is an investment that will pay for itself the very first time you are *not* late to a listing appointment in an unfamiliar area, or you decide to change routes to see a few more properties. I simply could not live without it — it saves me literally hours every day.

- Knowing that you don't have to worry about whether directions are right — even Mapquest gets it wrong sometimes — is a great stress reducer.
- All I have to do is touch the "Home" icon, and I'm on my way home.

7. Power. You depend on your laptop or tablet PC, your multi-function phone, your camera, and other electronic devices. What do you do when there is a power outage? What do you do when you are nowhere near an outlet where you can plug in your device charger?

- Extra batteries are worth the weight and investment; they are as important a tool as the electronics themselves. I have extra computer batteries, camera batteries, and any other batteries I need to keep going.

- I also carry a variety of connectors so that I can plug in to things other than a conventional wall outlet. With the right connector, I can run my laptop off the cigarette lighter in my car, on a train, or in a plane.

8. Video. In just a few short years we've gone from sending film away to be developed, to having instantly visible digital photos, to video on demand for our Websites and our blogs. As this is written, the newest favorite toy of real estate people seems to be the Flip Video camera. This camcorder is small, simple to use, and includes software and a USB connector to make sharing and downloading simple.

- If photographs help connect you to potential clients, video can help connect with motion and sound. Many blogging platforms now include the ability to add videos to your articles, and a well-done video can enhance your Website.
- Videos can be effective if your clients are in the generation that lives on Facebook and surfs on YouTube. You can showcase listings, do a testimonial, or do an interview on a blog, all with the video.
- Remember that if you do choose to add videos to your emails, blogs, and Website, don't limit yourself to just videos; not everyone wants to communicate that way, and you still need words and still pictures to reach the widest audience.

9. Techy tools. These are the little things that make a big difference. One of my favorites, and one I've had for years, is a sonar measuring device. This can be a real "Wow!" factor on listings. With it you can measure room sizes and avoid wrestling with a tape measure. I use it with sellers all the time: sometimes I'll let them take the room measurements while I make notes, other times I'll hand them my tablet PC and let them write on it while I do the measuring. Either way, I'm involving them in the process and solidifying the listing.

10. Groups. Much of what I've learned about technology has come because I joined and became active in groups that focus on the use of technology in real estate. I'm part of several groups that connect through listservs. These private mailing lists let a group communicate with other members. They also have regular seminars and Webinars as group benefits.

Even though as real estate agents we meet new people all the time, we still need a base of colleagues with whom we can share information and ideas.

- CyberStars®: Created by Allen Hainge, the CyberStars® are leading sales associates in their marketplaces. Each one uses today's technology to the fullest, and twice each year they gather as a group to share information on how they build their businesses, trade tips and techniques on using the latest technology, and network in order to build a money-making referral base. I've made great friendships, and I really would not be able to work as a solo agent at the level I do without all the knowledge I've gained and the support I can call on from my fellow CyberStars®.
- CyberProfessionals™: CyberProfessionals™ are leaders in using technology and sharing marketing ideas in the real estate industry. The group meets twice a year in different locations around the United States, and if you are serious about sharing and learning the high

end of current technology in a "non-geek" casual environment, then this might be the group for you. Every time I go to a CyberProfessionals™ meeting, I learn something new while reconnecting with colleagues from all over the country.

- ACRE™: Mollie Wasserman founded the ACRE™ Course and Coaching Program for the Accredited Consultant in Real Estate designation. The idea behind earning the ACRE™ designation is being able to give my clients choices about what services they receive when buying or selling real estate. An experienced real estate professional knows the market, knows what works, and knows how to sell a home. My clients get the benefit of all this experience and knowledge even if we never get to a transaction. But sometimes, someone isn't looking to sell their home and just needs some good solid advice, how do I help that person? That's where ACRE™ allows me to consult on an hourly basis so that the person gets the needed help, and I am compensated for the time and expertise I've spent years developing.

- Core Values Club: This group was created and designed by Floyd Wickman as a support system and follow up for his S.M.A.R.T. Selling. Through continuous "arms length" contact with Floyd, the Floyd Wickman Team, and other students, Core Values Club Members remain focused, motivated, and on track toward achieving their long range goals.

As helpful as technology is to my business, I have found an unexpected extra low-tech benefit: It helps make connections in person. I was once in Boston for personal reasons, and I wondered who might be in the same area. I did a search and found that Jack Peckham, founder of RECS (Real Estate Cyberspace Society), was not only in the same city, he was in the same zip code. So I called him, and he asked where I was staying. When I told him, he said, "Look out your window. That's my building." We met in person and made a great connection.

That dynamo Joeann Fossland is another example. While in New Mexico at Canyon Ranch with Lee, I found that we were not far from her. So I called her, we met for dinner, and a great friendship and mutual admiration society began.

The point is, technology gives us plenty of tools to make our work faster and more efficient, but we can never lose sight of the human connection that is so important to long-term success.

What if you don't think technology is for you?

All I can say is…think again. Remember that more than 80 percent of buyers start their search for a home and a real estate agent by going to the Internet. Email is a standard means of communication, right up there with the telephone. Your identity as a real estate professional is as much formed by your Website and blog as it is by your business cards and print advertising. Your clients and your competition are online; you need to be, too.

So what can you do to ease your discomfort? Start simply. Talk to colleagues, take the e-PRO® course, and add components as you can. Get the basics in place — computer, multi-function phone, Website — then expand as you become comfortable with these. Join Active Rain, where you'll find loads of advice and read the stories of people who have been where you are. Ask lots of questions, and choose what works for you.

Try to find someone like Allen Hainge. He has given me a great deal in my career, starting with his confidence in my ability when he invited me to be a CyberStar® and asked me to write a chapter in his book. Back then I was still a novice about technology, but he took me into his group of highly tech-savvy professionals. When we get together as a group, I still feel like the new kid with so much to learn. But the CyberStars® are like Allen himself — encouraging, giving, sharing people.

When you update your tech tools, do it because you'll improve efficiency or customer service, not just because there's something new on the market. Remember to ask, **What's Important Now?"** What you invest in becoming techno-savvy will pay dividends many times over in your business.

Planning and choosing your technology

Obviously, technology plays a huge role in my business. One of the advantages of working solo is that I only have to plan for my own needs. This way I can react to what's happening not only in my market but also in the very important rest of my life with family and friends. I'm a believer in living in the moment; this doesn't mean I don't plan, but it's not the top of the list. When it comes to technology I react to what I need, not to what new technogadget is coming out next.

The question to ask yourself is not, "What can this technology tool do for me?" You should be asking, "What do I need help with? What's slowing me down or making it hard for me to accomplish? What's wasting my time?" Once you know where the bottleneck in your day is, then you can look for a tool that will help you around it. It's very easy to be seduced by the "cool" features of computers and cameras and phone/PDAs. But if you have to wrestle with the tool to get what you need, it's not helping.

We are Realtors®. We list and sell houses. That's what we do, and I believe in delegating tasks that slow me down; I delegate a lot to technology. All of these tools suit my style. Because I work solo, I have to work smarter, and the technology tools help me do that.

After the recap, it's on to the important task of keeping up with the industry.

CHAPTER NINE – TECH SAVVY OR GADGET ADDICT?
❑ Technology won't make you better at listing and selling houses, but it will help you do what you do faster and more efficiently.
❑ Choose technology tools that solve a problem for you and your business; it doesn't have to be the "latest and greatest" to be the best thing for you. The best one for you is the one you will use.
❑ To be a top real estate professional today, you must find and use technology that improves your ability to reach and communicate with your clients, prospective buyers and sellers, and your colleagues.

TEN
KEEPING UP AND GETTING AHEAD

Have you ever come to the end of the weekend, exhausted, looked at a pile of paperwork and wondered, "I've been running so fast; how could I be so far behind?" Things you want to do for your business and for your career get pushed aside in the crush of listings, showings, contracts, and settlements. You hear about a course you'd like to take to get a new designation, but where will you find the time?

If this sounds too familiar, you are not alone. That doesn't make it any easier, of course, but we all deal with balancing the pressures of business with the pull of family. And somehow, we have to take the time to keep up with our changing industry, to keep improving our ability to provide the quality of service we give our clients.

Make the right choice for you

What to do? First, figure out how to hand off some of those business chores you have been doing yourself. Go back and re-read Chapter 7 if you need to. Find ways to give yourself breathing room.

Then you're ready to consider how you can improve your client service. Ask yourself some questions:

- What do I like best about real estate?
- What do I want to learn about?
- What kind of client do I like to work with most?
- What's my learning style?
  Visual — I learn best by reading the material, such as on a computer screen or in a book.
  Auditory — I learn best by hearing the material, such as on an audio tape or CD, a Webinar, or by teleseminar.
  Independent — I learn best on my own, at my own pace.
  Interactive — I learn best in a structured situation such as a classroom or a group of real estate professionals.
- When do I learn best — early in the morning or later in the day?
- Where do I learn best? Do I prefer to stay in town for seminars, or go out of town where I can network with other Realtors® for referrals?

Once you have these answers, you'll be on your way to choosing your next area of continuing study and advanced designation. That's when the fun starts.

There are literally dozens of courses you can take and certifications or designations you can earn. If you're new to the real estate business, you probably don't have any idea what all those letters after a Realtor®'s name are. I certainly didn't before I got into the business — they were just so much alphabet soup. But they are important because they can tell you a lot about the person's training and proven ability.

That alphabet soup after my name can be confusing, and we'll get to sorting the letters in a moment. But first, you'll recall that there are two letters you won't see that refer to part of my life that has an enormous influence on who I am today and how I work with my clients. Those letters are R.N.

My earlier life was as a registered nurse — a pediatric nurse in fact — and the youngest Head Nurse of Pediatrics and the Outpatient Department at Sinai Hospital in Baltimore. The people skills I learned through formal training and on the job are at the core of who I am today. I learned to understand what people needed even if they didn't or couldn't tell me. I learned that a small gesture of caring can be just what someone needs to get through a difficult time. And I learned that kind deeds circle around and come back to you tenfold.

Listing and selling houses is a different world from the life-and-death reality of a metropolitan hospital. But people still need expert help, assurance, and kindness. You won't find R.N. in my alphabet soup, but it's there in everything I do.

Now to decode some real estate designations for you as we go through my list so far:

- **ABR** — Accredited Buyer Representative, for real estate professionals focusing on all aspects of buyer representation.
- **CRS®** — Certified Residential Specialist, REALTORS® who complete advanced training in listing and selling, and meet rigorous production requirements.
- **e-PRO®** — Internet Certification by the National Association of REALTORS® for online professionalism.
- **GRI** — Graduate, REALTOR® Institute of the National Association of REALTORS® for NAR members involved in residential real estate who want a solid base of information for their practice.
- **LTG** — Leadership Training Graduate of the Women's Council of REALTORS®.
- **PMN** — Performance Management Network designation by the Women's Council of REALTORS®, a new

designation reflecting the idea that in order to enhance your business, you must enhance yourself, with training in: negotiating strategies and tactics, networking and referrals, business planning and systems, personal performance management and cultural differences in buying and selling.

- **RECS** — Real Estate CyberSpace Specialist designation of the Real Estate CyberSpace Society. This certification lets clients know you are proficient in serving the public with recognized skills for utilizing CyberSpace marketing programs and for effectively adopting special technology and networking systems. (I am also the Chair of the Baltimore Chapter.)

- **RRC** — Referral and Relocation Certification from the Women's Council of REALTORS® as a specialist in the area of relocation.

- **SRES®** — Seniors Real Estate Specialist designation trains REALTORS® to profitably and ethically serve the real estate needs of clients age 50+.

- **CyberStars®** — Allen F. Hainge CyberStars® meet high standards of professionalism, technology use, and client service. There are more than 4 million real estate agents but only 200 CyberStars®. Each CyberStar® is a proven leader in their market.

- **CyberProfessionals™** are leaders in using technology and sharing marketing ideas in the real estate industry.

- **ACRE™** — Accredited Consultant in Real Estate. I'm very proud to have been the first in Baltimore to earn the ACRE certification. ACRE gives me the option to offer consulting on an hourly basis as an alternative to a traditional commission arrangement. My clients can choose what's best for them, and I am compensated for my time and the expertise I've developed over more than 18 years in real estate.

- **CAP** — Certified Auction Professional is a designation for non-auction professionals that is intended to prepare them to deal with all facets of the auction industry in an ethical and compassionate manner.

Some of these designations I earned because I felt they were necessary for building my business. GRI, LTG, PMN, and RRC are in that category. Others came about with my growing technology habit: e-PRO, RECS, CyberStars, CyberProfessionals. And I earned the ACRE accreditation because I always want to offer my clients as many options as possible.

Can I point to measurable increases in my income thanks to each of these designations? Maybe. But has earning them given me more tools to serve my clients, and more ways to expand my business? Absolutely! Your business is a living thing, and you need to feed it constantly with new ideas and new information. Once you get into the learning mode, you may find an unexpected benefit; you get a shot of energy and enthusiasm from investing in yourself. Even if it's just for a few hours, that detachment from the everyday can help you recharge.

Which brings me full circle to how I learn best; to a Type E, "best" means "the fastest, most time-effective way." For me, that's audiotapes or CDs that I listen to in the car. Sure, I love a good class or seminar where I can network with others, but for pure learning and being able to really focus, my time alone on the road is the most valuable. Early in my career, I had Floyd Wickman's courses on tape and almost always had one running in the car. It got to where, when the tape deck needed cleaning it meant I had gone about 3,000 miles, which reminded me that I also needed an oil change. (Yes, that's also a Type E way of keeping track; it works much better for me than those little plastic stickers on the windshield!)

Keeping at it

How is real estate like poker? "It takes minutes to learn the game and a lifetime to master it." It's true of poker, and I think it is also true of real estate and many other professions.

My friend who is a personal trainer saw Oprah interviewing someone who lost lots of weight and used a personal trainer to help get her back in shape. The newly slim woman loved the trainer so much and praised the way she helped her. Not satisfied to just tout the wonderful talents of the trainer, she decided to take a few courses, learn how to train others, and become that person who gets accolades. She wanted to be a personal coach, helping people to change their lives by losing weight and exercising.

Her intention was good. But with little training herself, the chance of her hurting people through inexperience is much greater than of helping them. Intentions do not make you an expert. Watch a professional ice skater glide across the ice, spin, and leap. Then watch an amateur and see how hard it is. Years of practice, study, and training, are needed before you can make it look easy.

I have found that many buyers and sellers decide to go into real estate after their own transaction. They think, "So much money for doing so little" — or so it seems. I have dozens of clients who have gotten their real estate licenses because I made it look so easy. Many times I meet these new agents in classes that I am speaking at or attending. They are surprised. Why is an established agent still going to these seminars? Too often, they just don't get it, that making it look easy takes years of practice and experience along with continual learning.

How many of these former clients have made a success in real estate? How many have even made it through the first year? How many have sold the house that I helped them buy within that year? How many have blamed the poor market on not being a success? I think you can guess.

Many people can take the classes, pass the exam, and do all the things an agent "is supposed to do." But no matter what new technology or sure-fire system you want to try, there is still nothing like good old, roll-up-your-sleeves experience. It takes time and effort to acquire, but you can see the dividends in loyal clients, repeat business, and income that reflects all that hard work.

Next, we'll reap the rewards of all that hard work with referrals and repeat business.

CHAPTER TEN – KEEPING UP AND GETTING AHEAD
❏ Your real estate education does not stop when you get your license; lifelong learning will help your business grow.
❏ Make it part of your business plan this year to earn at least one new designation that fits with your interests and learning styles.
❏ A successful real estate career doesn't happen overnight; give yourself time to learn the moves and build your business for the long run.

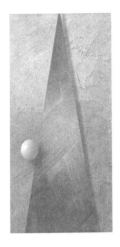

ELEVEN
YOUR BEST KIND OF BUSINESS

There's a well-known saying in both retail and wholesale business-es that it's easier to get new orders from an existing customer than it is to get an order from someone who has never dealt with you before. That just makes sense; if you are honest and ethical in your business, people will want to keep buying from you.

The thing is, this is also true for real estate, even though that repeat sale may not come for many years. And like most other things in real estate and in business in general, it's all about build-ing relationships, and not only with the people who list with you. Sometimes it's the person on the other side of the transaction who remembers what it was like to deal with you and calls you the next time they are ready to buy. That's exactly what happened a couple of years ago for me.

One day I received this email (used with permission):

"Dear Mrs. Rome,
I don't know if you remember me. My name is Kaliq Simms, and about six months ago, we happened to be getting gas at the same station on Reisterstown Rd. [in Baltimore]. I recognized your name on your license plate. You had been

the seller's Realtor® for a house we contemplated buying about six years ago when we were shopping for our current home.

I was so impressed with your professionalism and great personality. We ended up buying another home (no fault of yours, of course), but I continued to visit your Website periodically over the years, as I knew we would eventually want to sell our current starter home. Long story short, you gave me your number at the gas station that day and told me to call you when we decided to sell. Well, we've decided :)!

I hope we can work together. We need a speedy and smooth sale because we have found the house we want to buy. We are already pre-qualified and have a Realtor® for the buy-side of this transaction. Please call us as soon as possible. Thank you!"

That Saturday I went on a listing appointment, and though they said they absolutely wanted to use me, they also said they wanted their attorney to look over the listing agreement. I told them, "Absolutely, and here is what he'll say: He'll tell you the commission is too high and the term is too long, and that you shouldn't sign it."

While they were waiting to hear from the attorney, as a surprise for this delightful young family I put their home on my Website with no address, no price, and a "Coming Soon!" heading. Later that week they reported that the lawyer said exactly what I predicted, but after thinking it over some more, they listed their home with me anyway.

I knew that this would be a lovely experience because Kaliq had impressed me when we had met before. Sure enough, Kaliq and Joe were a delight to work with. They were sensible about pricing and recognized that the market was not the same as it had been a year before. We set a price that gave them what they wanted, and quickly had several showings. In just about a week we had a contract!

When we settled, like everything else about dealing with Kaliq and Joe, it was smooth and pleasant. Everyone left the settlement table feeling good. Transactions like this are what keep my business strong no matter the market, and why I deal almost exclusively with referrals. I know that Kaliq and Joe will call me when they are ready to move again, and that they will tell their friends and family, too.

I've said it before: Real estate is more than sticks and bricks. It is about people, it is about relationships, and it's about doing the right thing all the time. When you invest time and effort in building your network, you are laying the groundwork for future success.

One of the best measures of your success is how much appreciation you get from clients. My husband says I work for thank you notes and I have to agree; I like them better than any paycheck. Hard to believe? Here's a good example.

Dear Margaret:

We find it amazing that we never got around to thanking you for all of your effort in selling our home of over 41 years.

Phyllis and I were talking about a range of things last night, and the conversation came up about some friends who could not understand why we did not try to sell the house ourselves in such an active market, or use one of the discount Realtor® services. Everyone seems to have stories of houses sold to the first prospect, even before the "For Sale" sign went into the ground.

I guess some people feel that they must squeeze every last dollar that they can get, but perhaps they fail to recognize that there is not only the price, there is a cost. I question whether or not the cost of doing it yourself is worth it?

In looking back we had no idea what a realistic asking price should be, how long our house might be on the market, and what improvements, beyond a new roof, we might have needed as a result of inspections. Unknowns for us, but not for you.

We would have been more than a bit overwhelmed and crazy with the appointment process, the last-minute cancellations, the no-shows, etc. Not to mention answering the prospective buyers' questions about every appliance, the heating system, the windows, the plumbing, the electrical system, the ceiling, the fireplace, the "chimley," and of course, what kind of floors are under the carpeting. We had confidence in you, so we just let you do the work, and thank you for doing so.

You gave us an appropriate level of guidance, you emphasized "curb appeal," and you reminded us that we still had to live in the house while it was for sale. I think you implied that a prospective buyer and/or their Realtor® would recognize this fact. Our not being present allowed the prospects to look where they wanted to look, ask the questions that they wanted to ask, and to voice their opinions, concerns and objections to you freely.

Hindsight is often "20-20." But as we look back we truly had no idea about how to sell our home.

Our experience convinced us that sellers should always use a knowledgeable Realtor® when selling their property. The right Realtor® will do their best to make the process as trouble free as possible, save you loads of time, and get you the best price that they can.

> *That, Margaret, is precisely what you did, and we sincerely thank you.*
>
> *Phyllis and Mort, July 20, 2006*

When I speak with young agents, I tell them, "Do every single thing with the hope of getting a thank-you note. When they start coming in, the money will follow." Repeat customers and referrals can quickly become the core of your business when you focus on what's best for your client and what you can do to bring it about. The warm note of thanks you receive from your clients will make that commission check look even better.

What makes people send thank-you notes?

Think about what it's like to move. I don't know anyone who enjoys it. Buying a new home is exciting, selling the old house is stressful, packing is a pain, and the actual moving looms as a headache the size of Mt. Everest. What can you do to make it a better experience for your clients?

Short of doing the work for them, what you can do is provide them with suggestions and advice about dealing with the often conflicting emotions surrounding such a big life change. This is one of those times when my experience in nursing comes to the surface. When you are a nurse you learn as much about psychology as about medicine, and that's handy for a real estate agent. One thing I've found helpful is reminding people that the emotions will be strong, and that they need to give those feelings time to be expressed. I shared this with a woman who was having an especially hard time recognizing that parting is such sweet sorrow.

> *Have you ever had to say "good-bye" to a close and dear friend? Can you imagine how sad you would feel if you*

> *were never going to see that friend again and did not have a chance to say good-bye?*
>
> *Everyone knows that moving from one home to another takes a lot of time, planning, and emotion. You work hard getting the house ready to show and sell, and then even harder sorting and packing. You have friends and neighbors you won't see any more after you move, and you need to take time to say your farewells to them. What no one talks about is the last step, the final good-bye that you need to say…to your house.*
>
> *The home you are leaving is part of you no matter whether you've spent 5 months or 85 years living there. Each room holds memories of people, events, happy times, and not-so-good times. Just as you need to say good-bye to people so you can move on to the next phase in your life, so you also need to say good-bye to the home that has sheltered you.*
>
> *Take a few minutes in each room, think about the things that happened there, acknowledge them, cry or laugh if that's what you feel, and say your farewell. It's a kind of grieving, and you must get emotional closure. You invested more than just money in your home; you invested yourself. Give yourself time to say good-bye.*

Moving with children has its own special challenges. Families often choose to move to a new home during the summertime so their children can feel at home in the new place before school starts. It makes good sense to give kids the chance to settle in before taking on the challenges of a new school, no matter what their ages.

When I have clients with children, I share with them these tips for making the move easier on children from my very special clients, Keith and Kim Holmes, who have lots of experience and wisdom on the subject.

- Most importantly — LISTEN. Children will give you all kinds of signs. Take care to be in tune with their feelings, fears, and concerns.

- Be sure to involve them, especially in decisions that affect them. Let them choose carpet color and paint for their room. For younger children you can offer several choices you like and let them choose their favorite; older kids can have more latitude. Ask for their advice on things like a new mailbox or trash cans for the new house.

- Be sensitive to their wishes. The adults will have hour-on-hour of "new house" discussions, but there will be times when the children just don't want to take part.

- Give them a timetable to help them understand when the move will take place. When you know the date for sure, tell your kids, and circle it on a "new house" calendar. Then plan activities and events they can participate in leading up to the big day.

- Take your child to the new house as often as possible before the move so it becomes a familiar place.

- Always talk about the move in a positive way. Share information, but be careful that you don't overload your children with too much. Help them see the fun in the move. Make sure that it's clear to them that their stuff from the old house comes to the new house.

Selling your house and buying a new home is stressful even when it's a wonderful move for everyone. Helping your children to be comfortable with the move will also take some of the stress off you.

Offering advice and support are important and can make the difference between something being just a deal and the start of a life-long relationship of sales and referrals. In the end, it comes down to how you do business. It's easy to talk about "going the extra mile" and "thinking outside the box." One of the best ways to know if you are really doing these things is not to look at your checkbook but to look at your mailbox. You'll never have to worry about that checkbook when you get letters like this:

> *Two and one-half years ago I put my gorgeous property on the market...and the entire process is indeed a story to tell.*
>
> *Margaret Rome was not my first real estate agent, but was referred to me by a mutual friend who felt that she was the most capable and did outstanding marketing. Margaret had been a ceramic artist herself (as am I) and we hit it off right away. She saw the beauty and special magic in my home and studio and was excited by the endless possibilities other agents did not see.*
>
> *There was extensive advertising (NY Times, Washington Post, Style Magazine, local newspapers, Margaret's radio show and every relevant internet site, etc.). There were radio interviews, articles, networking; there was even a contest for the most creative use of my historic home/church/studio and the winners were announced on the radio show.*
>
> *I worked with Margaret Rome who was focused and audacious. My property was on a prime corner in a very affluent area of Howard County — a historic property that required a special buyer. My new studio was up and running in New Mexico, and I simply could not sustain two properties any more. After much discussion, Margaret brought up the idea of an auction. Her rationale was that we could have much better signage, and create buyer frenzy. We had*

two interested buyers but they could not make the final de-cision; they wanted to wait out the market.

Thinking "outside the box" always takes courage and it was Margaret that first opened the option of AUCTION. I discovered that by having a partnership of auctioneer/real estate agent, I was getting the best of both worlds. I did not have to deal directly with the auction house; Margaret was my spokesperson and I was kept informed.

My property did sell at auction and the settlement took place in the 30 days as promised. Everything was done and coordinated and I was able to sign the deed prior to the clos-ing day, even in a difficult real estate market. I was kept in the loop via email and phone. The day of the auction, it was almost like being there. Communication lines were kept open throughout this entire process.

The lesson here is that "going by the book" may work some of the time, but, for me, imagination and courage were the ticket. Wish I had opted for the auction route sooner!

Tatiana

Sure, I got paid for the transaction. But I treasure this note from a woman who became first a client and then a friend. For me, it doesn't get any better than this.

Doing business with friends and family

One of the things new agents are often warned about is doing business with friends and family. Just like the old warning about not borrowing money from a family member or friend because of what that can do to a relationship, people seem to think that being a friend's real estate agent is trouble waiting to happen.

That is so far away from what I believe. If you know I'm your friend and will do my best for you, why in the world would you want to go to someone else who doesn't care about you? If you know how I work with people who are not friends, then why would you think I would do any less for you? If we are friends, then we will both go into a real estate relationship expecting the same level of courtesy and honesty that we put into our friendship. It's true that you should not use somebody as your agent just because they're a friend, but why would you *not* use them if they are the best in the business?

So there you have it. We've talked about the real estate business from first listing to working by referral only. You know how I've built a successful solo business over more than 18 years, and what I've learned along the way. Time to wrap it up with one last topic: having a life!

CHAPTER ELEVEN – YOUR BEST KIND OF BUSINESS
❑ Real estate is more than sticks and bricks; it's about people. How you treat them will determine your level of success.
❑ Do everything you can to earn thank-you notes from clients; money will follow the gratitude, as will referrals and repeat business.
❑ You can do business with friends and family because you will treat them with the same respect and honesty as someone you just met.

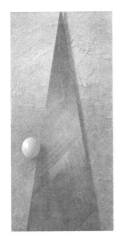

TWELVE
YOUR LIFE IN REAL ESTATE

Yes, you can have a "normal" life and be a successful real estate professional. In fact, you *must* have a life outside real estate if you want to reach those million-dollar marks in your profession. It is so easy to get caught up in the details and pressures of listings, showings, and settlements, that you can find yourself working seven days a week and taking client phone calls at all hours of the day and night.

Don't do it. This is your profession, but the rest of your life makes it possible to be good at what you do. If you sacrifice family time and personal time by devoting yourself to your business, you can't guarantee that your business will benefit in the long term, but you can be sure that you and your family will suffer. Think of what they say on an airplane: "Put on your own oxygen mask first and then help those who need it."

Now having said that, I don't mean that you can't combine personal and business time successfully. I do it all the time!

One day I decided to take some time away from real estate and reconnect with my inner artist. The Baltimore Clayworks was hosting a panel discussion with international artists in connection with a gallery exhibition. It sounded like the perfect couple of hours — for this former ceramic artist — completely removed from listing and selling.

So there I was on a Sunday afternoon at a nearby conference center for a lecture/panel discussion that turned out a bit differently than planned. Two of the three panelists were unable to be there, so the one remaining brave soul led an open forum with the audience that turned into a lively discussion of women and art. In that lovely time bubble, homebuyers and sellers didn't exist.

Then it was back to Clayworks for the exhibition where I enjoyed that lovely earthy scent of the place where potters work. My real estate hat was firmly in place again by then and of course I talked about one of my special properties that was perfect for an artist. I met a teacher from a local college who knew one of my sellers, a dean at that college. And one person asked about houses in walking distance of Clayworks, which I happened to have, and who knows what might come of that?

The day reminded me of something we all know but is easy to forget: Do what you love. I went to the lecture because I love art and especially ceramic art. My past life as an artist is an important part of who I am and how I do my real estate business. I was there for the clay, and doing what I love was enough. But because I was there, I'll probably get more business.

This was another example of the importance of maintaining a positive attitude and always being on the lookout for ways to help people. I don't mean help them buy or sell a house. Just help because you can and because they need it. It's that Floyd Wickman's core principle: You *do* get by giving.

One of the things I enjoy most about real estate is helping people who really want to learn and who are trying to grow. When I get to stand up in front of a class and talk about the business, and find an enthusiastic agent who is listening to what I have to share, that's one of the best parts of real estate. If I can help them learn and be better agents, that can only make life better for all agents.

Do what you love. Your life — and business — will benefit.

Creating success

Don't be misled into thinking I'm just sitting around waiting to do nice things for people. Giving is important. But so is action. As my friend and teacher Anne Hruby says, "Real estate isn't the good life, it's the way to the good life. You can't sit around and wait for success to happen. You have to grab it and *make* it happen."

Sometimes you'll hear an agent say, "Oh, she's just lucky," about someone else's big sale. I don't believe in "luck" as something that just falls at your feet because you happen to be standing in the right place at the right time. My friend Toby Davis in Charleston, SC, sent me a story that really hit home — one of those "ah ha!" moments. At the same time, it reminded me about what it means to be lucky in real estate or in anything you do in life.

> *A teacher told his class of pottery students that he would grade half of them on the quantity of pots they produced, and the other half on the quality. In the Quantity group, it didn't matter how good or bad their results, only the total weight of pots they created would count. For the Quality group, all they had to have at the end of the semester was one perfect pot to get that A in the course.*
>
> *They set to work. The wheels whirled and the Quantity students turned out pot after pot, improving with each creation. On the other side of the room the Quality students thought and planned, and agonized every nuance of their creation. The strain of trying for perfection paralyzed many of them so that they ended up with nothing but unused lumps of clay.*

> *The moral? Good work is not perfect work. Not everyone you meet will be a client, and you won't sell every house you list. But if you keep meeting people and talking to prospects, you will find clients and even new friends.*

Those of you who know my background can understand why this got to me. I was that ceramic artist and I made lots and lots of pots, tried lots of new techniques, and learned a lot. Some pots were not so good and some were really, really good. Some I even tossed before they got to the kiln. But many pieces of ceramic art are in my home, and many more are decorating other homes and being enjoyed by friends and clients who own them.

Now I use this same approach in my real estate career.

- The more people I meet, the luckier I get.
- The more risk I take, the luckier I get.
- The harder I work, the luckier I get.

I have been very "lucky" in this wonderful world of real estate!

Common wisdom may be wrong

You know how it is. The newspapers and TV talk about how bad — or how good — the market is, and everywhere you go you hear people saying the same thing. It's the common wisdom, but that doesn't make it true for you. I saw proof of this early in my career when the real estate market was in a slump, or so I was told. Since I didn't know I couldn't list and sell houses, I did. And through the ups and downs of the market ever since, I've believed that if you think the real estate market is bad or good, you're right either way.

It's quite human to accept common wisdom as truth. It's easy to get caught up in the headlines of the day and forget that the people who write headlines are not in the business of helping to sell houses; they are in the business of writing headlines and stories that will get people to read them. "Real Estate Bubble Bursts!" will get much more attention than, "Things OK in Real Estate." What you need to be able to do is focus on the reality of your market, look at what's working or not, and then figure out what — if anything — to change about how you do business.

There are only three ways to cope with the situation you are in:

- Accept it.
- Change it.
- Leave it.

As a Realtor®, you can accept the market the way it is, but you can't change it, and as a career agent you can't leave it. So if it's a "bad" market, you deal with it.

Of course, a "good" or "bad" market depends on your perspective, doesn't it? Talk to the woman whose house just sold, and it's a great market. Talk to the man whose house has been on the market for a year, and it's a terrible market. The truth is, even in a "bad" market, you'll have houses that sell right away.

You know that real estate is a cyclical business. Spring and fall tend to be busier than the winter and summer. But the weather and the seasons don't make the time right or wrong; the best time to sell is when the seller is ready and is motivated to sell.

There are buyers' markets and sellers' markets, and they alternate. The important thing is not to get caught up in the scary statistics that the media will quote to show how very bad things are. The questions you need to answer are, "How are things in *my* market compared to a month or a year ago? Has the market changed, and if so, how?" And then take those answers and make the changes that will work for you.

Be careful of making decisions based on statistics you read or hear. Statistics are tricky. You can "prove" just about anything you like by quoting statistics, and many people will accept them as fact. When real estate professionals get together, you know that numbers and statistics will come up. With more than 1.24 million Realtors® [1](about half of all licensed real estate agents) selling about 4.34 million single-family homes a year[2], that works out to two sales a year for each real estate agent. I know I've done more than that, and so have many people I know, so there must be a lot of "agents" who are not selling anything!

This is a good example of why averages are useless. Even medians aren't much better. When you read that the median home price in the United States in 2007 was $219,000[3], you can bet that you can't find much of anything for that in Southern California, but in rural Louisiana it might buy quite a lot.

So recognize that averages make great headlines but they are meaningless. This applies to Realtors®, housing prices, time on market, weather, you name it. If one house in a town sells for $80,000 and another sells for $800,000, the average price is $440,000 — but that doesn't mean the owner of the $80,000 house will get more, or the other guy less. It doesn't change their individual situations. The go-getters among us will go and get, and they are at the top of the heap. In real estate and life, it's the individual who makes a difference. The people who got into real estate to make a quick buck are still sitting around waiting for those big checks. Soon they'll move on to some other "easy money" job and skew the averages on that one, too.

I'm so glad I'm not average!

---

1 National Association of REALTORS®, Membership Statistics, April 2008.
2 National Association of REALTORS®, Existing Single-Family Home Sales, April 2008
3 National Association of REALTORS®, Sales Price of Existing Single-Family Homes, Year 2007

Make it work for you

So what do you do if the real estate market isn't working for you? Focus in on you and your business, and take a good look at who and where your potential clients are and how best you can reach them. If you are in an area like Baltimore where there's been an increase in young singles buying in the renovated downtown areas, maybe that's where you need to shift some advertising efforts. If you are in an area where people are looking at retirement homes, perhaps you need to change your marketing to reach more Boomers. Whatever the situation, there are always options.

And there's one more thing: Do whatever it takes to give yourself that boost of confidence that can make the difference in a winning presentation. (Women will relate to what I'm about to say; guys, you'll have your own version.) Before a photo session for new headshots, I had my hair and makeup done professionally, and I felt absolutely terrific being photographed. That feeling showed in the photos, and I worked hard to remember that emotion. Later, I was able to connect that feeling to a pair of shoes that looked and felt great. They became my "kick-ass shoes," and whenever I put them on for a presentation, it brought back that confident feeling. In time, my ankle wore out and my high-heeled shoes were history, but the habit was ingrained, and I could pull up that "kick-ass shoes" feeling whenever I needed it, even if I was wearing running shoes.

Find your "kick-ass" feeling, and make it work for you.

Finding a balance

No, it's not easy finding that balance between building a successful career in real estate and keeping your family and friends as the important parts of your life that they are. Sometimes all the demands on you can seem overwhelming. How do you balance your family needs with the pressure of a settlement that is falling apart before your eyes? How do you choose between your spouse's important business dinner and presenting a contract on the largest sale of your career?

If the answer isn't immediately clear, go back and re-read page 15. It is the core of how I have managed to not only survive but also thrive as a solo agent throughout these years in real estate. WIN. **What's Important Now?** Those three words bring everything into perspective. What is the most important thing for you to do right this minute? If there are two that seem to be equally important, what happens if you choose one first and then the other? Can you do something quickly to support one option and then complete the other? You can't satisfy everyone all the time, but you must satisfy yourself that you have chosen the best solution at the time. WIN?

Once you've made that choice, whatever the consequences, move on. You can tear yourself up with "coulda-shoulda-didn't," but they do you no good. One of my earliest lessons in real estate came from a very wise, elderly lady. You read about her at the beginning of this book, in the introduction. She said, "Don't let unimportant people or unimportant things become important."

I was reminded of the story when I got a call from a very upset seller one day. She wasn't upset with me, or even that her wonderful house hadn't sold yet. It was something that had happened in her life, and because we had become friends, and because she felt she could talk to me, she unloaded. When she was done, I told her the story of that older lady; in fact, I have used this saying many times, and it always hits home. My seller quickly saw that the person who had upset her so was definitely in the *not* important category. So I urged her to give in to the desire to get all those things she wanted to say down in a scathing email, to send it to me, and then to look around at all the good things that have happened for her lately, and repeat after me: "*I don't do upset.*"

This principle is so important that I try to help my sellers in advance because I know that there will be something that goes wrong between the time we list their house and when we leave the settlement table. When they know that I'm there to help them through whatever happens, they can (hopefully) not panic when that glitch occurs. Since flying is part of my life, here's how I explain it:

You might call them potholes or bumps in the road or detours; I call them turbulence. All those things that can happen between the time you sign a contract to buy or sell a house, and the day the keys change hands at settlement.

So what is turbulence? It might be a contract with contingencies: You agree to sell your house to someone who has to sell their house in order to buy yours. That means your sale is contingent on their sale. What happens if your buyer is not able to sell? Oops — turbulence.

You find a house you love, that you just have to have. At first look you know it's a stretch for you financially, but it's the perfect house. Then you go back and crunch the numbers, adding in all the costs you didn't think about at first—closing costs, moving, new appliances, etc. Uh-oh — that house you love just became unreachable.

Or you are selling your home and have a buyer who looks perfect. They want your home, they offer full price, and sign a contract. Sounds great, but are they qualified, can they get the mortgage they need? If they don't, there's a pothole for you.

How do you handle these bumps? It's up to me to prepare you for them. My job as your Realtor® is to be honest with you from the start, to let you know that there will be

> turbulence. *When you are prepared and know that we will get past these bumps, you recognize them as normal and move on.*
>
> *Turbulence bounces you around, but a top professional Realtor® will help you get through the rough spots and on to a smooth settlement.*

Smooth settlements and happy landings

When it's all done, this is what we want for our clients and ourselves: A settlement that leaves everyone smiling; a successful sale for our clients; a new relationship of trust and respect for all parties; a feeling that we have made a positive difference for a family; and another client sending a glowing thank-you note to add that warm glow to the cold cash in our bank account.

That is doing *Real Estate the Rome Way!*

CHAPTER TWELVE – YOUR LIFE IN REAL ESTATE
❑ Always make time to do what you love and be with those you love. You cannot work in real estate 24/7 and be effective in the long term.
❑ Recognize that turbulence is part of the deal, and it's your job to help your clients weather the bumps through to a smooth landing.
❑ Always work for thank-you notes; the money will follow.

 **APPENDIX A**

PROFILE OF THE TYPE E PERSONALITY IN REAL ESTATE

To gain a better understanding of how Type Es operate in the world of residential real estate, and why they can be both a blessing and a curse to colleagues as well as family members, let's explore the quiz questions in more depth.

1. Do you love starting new projects, especially "impossible" ones?

Type Es are designed to create things, not run them. They crave new, exciting, never-been-done-before projects and impossible challenges. When someone says, "That house is impossible to sell," the Type E agent says, "Watch me!"

The fastest way to stress for a Type E is to get caught in a routine. Type Es need lots of room to create. They thrive in unconventional and unstructured environments that not only allow them to explore outside the box but also encourage them to do so.

2. Does the thought of having a 9-to-5 job make you break into a cold sweat?

Ask this of a Type E, and you can almost feel their panic. The typical 9-to-5 job is too restrictive and too repetitive for most Type Es. This is one reason why a career in real estate attracts Type E people. You set your own hours, you work when and where you want. Type Es must have control over their own lives and the freedom to quickly change direction as their agile minds see new opportunities and new ways of solving problems.

3. Do you quickly lose interest in a project or job once it is up and running?

Type Es need to be continually challenged. Creating something is a positive challenge. They thrive in this environment. But the minute the project they have been working on is up and running, they can lose interest.

In other professions, if the Type E doesn't have an exit strategy in place before this point, they will usually drive themselves and whatever they have created right into the ground. Seasoned Type Es in business will have a transition/management team all set to take over well before this point is reached.

This is another reason Type Es are naturally drawn to real estate — there is an automatic exit when the house is bought or sold. The Type E agent has the fun of creatively marketing the house, the challenge of doing it better than anyone else, and the satisfaction of seeing the transaction wrapped up at settlement.

The danger zone for real estate Type Es starts about three months after the listing if the market is slow and all the innovative marketing is not drawing attention. This is when a Type E agent goes off hunting new challenges and can lose interest in the one that isn't working.

4. Has delegating responsibility been a major challenge for you?

One of the most difficult hurdles for a Type E to overcome is allowing someone else to do a job. Type Es have the audacity to think that they can do the job better than anyone else. Unfortunately, they are usually right. Because they have a larger radarscope, greater intuition and heightened states of creativity, they really can get the job done better, faster and cheaper.

What they need is a reliable Type E translator to assist them. A Type E translator is a person or team that is bilingual. That is, they can speak Type E and effectively translate the Type E vision to other team members. At some point the Type E begins to realize that handing a project over to someone means it will usually get done to only 80 percent of perfection, but at least they will get their life back. They will be able to return to creating things instead of running them.

In a short-term real estate transaction, this is probably not necessary. But if a Type E wants to build a team or handle more listings, the hand-off of some tasks will be essential. For a real estate Type E, this can mean training someone else to write their ads or handle some follow-up calls. (See Chapter 7.)

5. When contacted by an old friend you haven't heard from in years, do you immediately pick up where you left off, as if no time has passed?

Unlike the short project, job, or relationship cycle that typical Type Es have, they tend to develop long and lasting friendships. While most people require time to reconnect with old friends they haven't been in contact with for years, Type Es have the ability to pick up right where they left off.

6. Do you love having time to yourself when you can find it?

Type Es need time to themselves. It is essential if they want to thrive not only personally but also professionally. This is one of the main differences between a type A and a Type E. Type As go 100 miles an hour but are afraid of stopping or of actually spending time with themselves. Type Es would love to have "alone" time, but are usually running with a schedule more suited to three people over the course of two lifetimes.

When I hear the weatherman calling for snow, I hope for a lot of snow, enough so that I'm snowed in and everyone else gets snowed out. When I was working in ceramics, I never worried about running out of milk on a snow day, only running out of clay.

7. Do you usually find small talk a waste of time?

Small talk, chit-chat and gossip are not the usual domain of the Type E personality. If they are going to engage in conversation, they need it to be meaningful, something with substance. One indication that a Type E is headed over the edge is that they will notice themselves beginning to gossip. Normally their projects and lives are much too engaging to leave them behind for lesser things.

This is another reason why you won't often see Type E agents hanging around the office or sitting down and talking on the phone. They won't be gossiping about the latest reality show because (a) they don't know what it is, and (b) even if they did, they wouldn't spend time watching it. If there are phone calls to be made, they'll make the calls from the car on the way to a listing or showing. Any small talk they engage in will be to ask you about your children or grandchildren.

8. Do most of your projects, jobs or romantic relationships usually last between six months to five years?

Most Type Es live with a six month to five-year project cycle in both their personal and professional lives. Once something is up and running, be it a job, business, or sometimes a relationship, they often lose interest. At this point, they will either head in a new direction within their present project, job, or relationship, or leave all together. If they fail to take action, they will find themselves stuck in the Critical Zone (see Appendix B), heading straight for a fall.

The beginning of a new project or relationship and its development is the most exciting phase for the Type E personality. They enter the Critical Zone as it nears the up-and-running phase. If they don't heed the four clear warning signs that they're heading for trouble, they will enter a state of seemingly perpetual crisis and eventually clinical depression.

The exception to this is, of course, when a Type E finds that one person who is their true love and partner for life. Because that relationship continually nourishes and supports, the Type E will invest every bit of love, caring, and effort in making it strong and lasting.

9. Did you grow up feeling that your view of life was different from that of most people?

A typical response from most Type Es is that there just weren't many other people who thought the way they did. They felt a bit odd. With only 5-10 percent of the population coming from a similar physiological point of view, that's not so surprising.

You will find that real estate is one field where you meet more than the usual 10 percent or so of Type Es. This is a profession made for the creative and enthusiastic Type E personality.

10. Do you consider yourself an intensely passionate person?

Passion and creativity are the hallmarks of the Type E personality. When they are tracking down the center line of their lives, immersed in creative endeavors with plenty of time to accommodate them, they are passion incarnate. Type Es carry that passion into every aspect of their lives, whether it's the boardroom or the bedroom or simply the indescribably delicious feeling of being alive.

 *Appendix B*

The Type E Critical Zone

One of the things successful Type Es do to support and nurture their unique personality is learn to recognize the four major warning signs of the Type E Critical Zone. Type Es have such a unique way of living and working in the world that they often find themselves in the midst of many problems with clients and other important relationships.

But these problems don't crop up overnight; they build over time, often unnoticed amid a flurry of activity, until one day the world seems to have come crashing down. Type Es who avoid the crash learn to heed the warning bells as they near the edge of the Type E Critical Zone.

1. Boredom. If you have a Type E personality, boredom is the first indication that you're approaching the Type E Critical Zone. Not surprisingly, it is one of the most difficult warning signs to detect because it occurs while you're busy. If the boredom is left unchecked, you unconsciously will turn your creative passion into a very passionate crisis for yourself and those you live and work with.

2. Worry. The second warning sign in the Type E Critical Zone is a dramatic increase in the time you spend worrying. Here's a tip: Write this down and place it where you will see it every day:

**Worry is nothing more than creativity
all dressed up with nowhere to go.**

Your creativity bounces about shouting excitedly, "Let's play! Let's play!" But you respond, "Sorry, I'm too busy right now." At that point, just like a two-year-old, your creativity goes looking for a problem to get your attention with. And it will find one.

3. The 2 a.m. wake-up call. Those who ignore the second warning sign will be blessed with warning number three — the 2 a.m. wake-up call. At this point you are solidly entrenched in running your project, even though you know you shouldn't. You will get a wake up call two to three hours after going to sleep, when your REM (rapid eye movement) or dreaming sleep, begins.

Since you have been too busy during the day to be creative, your brain jumps to life and, thinking you are ready to play, wakes you up. "Wow!" Your creativity shouts, "Am I glad to see you. I thought you'd never show up!" It then delightedly opens your eyes, ready for some fun.

If you're like most Type Es, you immediately look at the clock to see what time it is — as if that's going to make a difference. You know you're not going back to sleep anytime soon.

4. Crisis management. The fourth warning sign is that wherever you look, all you see is crisis. At some point, you realize that you've abandoned a life doing what you love for a job in crisis management. That's not a very smart trade, unless managing your own crises is what you love.

Don't make the mistake of trying to extricate yourself from the crises by attempting to solve them all. There's a common misperception that once everything is solved, you'll be able to return to your normal pattern of positive creativity. That goal is rarely reached. Unfortunately, such thinking just digs you deeper into the crisis mode because your focus is still on the problems which surround you, not on the opportunities.

 APPENDIX C

A TYPICAL TYPE E SOLUTION

A dozen years ago, I had an awful lot on my plate and was trying to balance everything. I was dealing with my mom having Alzheimer's while running a growing real estate business as a solo agent. One day my delightful husband inquired about my checking account. Now, you need to understand that Lee is a Wharton School graduate, and his checkbook balances to the penny — always.

"Your checkbook is a mess," he said. "You have no idea how much money you have."

My answer, of course, was, "Sure I do. It's within a couple thousand dollars." You can imagine the exasperated look on his face.

He said, "If you reconcile your account, I will take it over."

I'm not sure that he even figured I heard what he said. But the next day I looked at my checkbook to find the address of the bank; how else would I ever know where it was located? I went into the bank and said, "Please close this account and open a new one."

I returned home and placed the brand new reconciled checkbook on my husband's desk. There was that exasperated look again, but I think also a wee bit proud. I did what he asked. The checkbook was balanced and reconciled. I just did it differently than he would. It made sense to me. I could have spent hours, days, even weeks adding, subtracting, entering, and deleting. But in the end I felt the bank would be right, so why should I do it? My time is much more valuable.

I have told this story many times. In fact, when I speak to groups it is one of my favorite ways of explaining time management and how I am able to work without an assistant. It's always interesting to see the reactions. Some people laugh and applaud, while others say, "Oh, my, you could have cost yourself hundreds of dollars!" But I believe this is the way a Type E thinks.

And yes, Lee still does take care of my account. I use the checks that create a copy when one is written, so everything he needs is there. It's wonderful that I don't even have to think of this task any more.

Oh, and while I was delegating...I no longer open my mail, either.

ABOUT THE AUTHOR

What can you say that sums up a person who sells homes at full price or better, who earns a full commission rate, who has people waiting to list with her, who is electronically connected in every way imaginable, who schedules time off regularly, and who manages to be a nice person at the same time?

Two words: Margaret Rome.

After successful careers as a pediatric nurse and a ceramic artist, Margaret Rome found her niche in real estate in 1990. This award-winning dynamo began her real estate career in the Baltimore area, and that market has never been the same.

Margaret chooses to work alone with no staff or assistants, and limits the number of listings she takes at any one time so that she can give each client the very personal attention that generates future referrals. She has developed time and energy management techniques that help her to be a consistent top producer.

Margaret has enthusiastically embraced the technology tools that help to serve her clients quickly, effectively, and personally. Her Web site is a valuable tool where buyers and sellers can learn about her properties, read about her accreditations, certifications, and awards, and see testimonials from delighted clients. She is in demand as a speaker at conferences and is a frequent guest and host of the weekly radio program, "All About Real Estate."

Her tag line says it all:

Sell Your Home with Margaret Rome.

Index

K

"kick-ass" – 165
Kappleman, Murray – 63

L

Lee – 16, 17, 39, 51, 138, 177, 178
lender – 33, 83, 85, 86, 87, 88
license
  real estate license – 5, 10, 11, 12, 22, 23, 35, 49, 104, 147, 149
listing agent – 30, 31, 50, 71, 112
listing presentation – 1, 55, 57
logo – 46
LTG – 143, 145
lucky – 23, 161, 162

M

M&Ms – 91, 117
Madzel, Malynda – 41
marketing – 2, 35, 40, 45, 47, 74, 104, 107, 108, 117, 118, 119, 122, 123, 132, 136, 144, 156, 165, 170
Maryland – 6, 7, 15, 27, 114, 118, 121
Master Sales Academy. – 24
mentor
  mentoring – 25, 26, 84, 117
MLS – *See* multimple list
Montillo, Lauren – 104
multiple list – 28, 45, 67, 68, 109, 120
multiple listing service – *See* multiple list

Printed in the United States
207728BV00001B/151-1524/P